The Correct Thing
for Catholics

BY
LELIA HARDIN BUGG
&
COLLEEN HAMMOND

Originally published: by:

NEW YORK, CINCINNATI, CHICAGO

Benziger Brothers

Printers to the Holy Apostolic See

Copyright 1891 by Benziger Brothers

ISBN: 978-0-9845075-5-9

Reprinted by Valora Media, Inc

Cover and layout: Colleen M. Hammond

Copyright 2014 by Valora Media, Inc.

Printed in the United States of America

THIS

LITTLE BOOK

IS HUMBLY INSCRIBED

TO

Saint Joseph

IN GRATITUDE FOR SIGNAL FAVORS

RECEIVED THROUGH

HIS INTERCESSION

MARCH 22, 1891

L. H. B.

Being a collector of antique books, somewhere along the line I picked up this volume of *The Correct Thing for Catholics*, by Miss Lelia Hardin Bugg. The receipt tucked in the front cover indicated that I had actually ordered a different book, and the seller accidentally shipped me this one. I now recall stowing this handbook away — knowing that someday I'd get back to it.

That 'someday' was a couple of months ago. Cleaning out a cupboard, something drew my eye to the crumbling 133-year-old leather spine, and my eyes fixed on the title. "Correct thing," I thought. "What *is* the correct thing?"

As I scanned through the pages, I realized that nearly every tidbit of the author's advice that was applicable in 1881 is still true today. Baptisms. Waiting in line for confession. Approaching for Communion. Confirmation issues. Visiting convents. The correct thing for when a priest arrives in your home for a sick call. Funerals. Engagements. Weddings.

But it's not just the Sacraments. Miss Bugg also touches on Catholics in public. Politics. At home. In business. And even the correct thing when traveling.

It's only when you stumble across a few obvious exceptions — a man shot in a duel, separate sides of the confessional for men and women, how to treat servants, paying for a priest's horse or carriage fare — that you are jolted back into the present. You may even be comforted by the idea that common sense wasn't all that 'common' a century ago, either.

A little warning. Be prepared to be taken aback by some of the local customs mentioned, the stringency of Lenten requirements a century ago, and changes in Sacramental preparations. However, in the interest of our rich heritage and Faith, the original text has been left virtually as it was written. (Please consult your parish priest for details on current practices.)

This book provides a robust bounty of proper behaviors and etiquette that are timeless. And timeless is what Catholic novelist Lelia Hardin Bugg was hoping for. I can imagine her consulting with and interviewing the priests she knew in her hometown of Wichita, Kansas who shared with her, "the ignorance and thoughtlessness, of the blunders, ludicrous and annoying when not serious" that they encountered in their parishes. I'm sure if you sat down with your parish priest today, he might share similar frustrations — how parishioners are either uninformed or unconcerned about the correct thing to do.

Lelia Hardin Bugg wrote in her preface that she hoped that her little book would, "fill a long-felt want" long after the copyright had expired. Re-publishing her work now is an attempt to fulfill her hope — to bridge time and bring her little volume into the 21st century.

Thank you, Lelia. 133-years later, we feel that your work *does* fill a long-felt want.

Colleen M. Hammond
Easter Monday, April 21, 2014

These pages aim, to a limited extent, to be at once a guide for the exterior conduct of Catholics on some of the occasions where there is a liability of annoying mistakes, and a reminder of obligations understood but often times forgotten.

In a country where Catholics in certain crude communities are still regarded with suspicion and dislike, and where even in more cultivated centers the clouds yet linger of ignorance and hereditary prejudice, Catholics are doubly bound to bring no reproach on the grand old Church. We are judged not as individuals but as Catholics; therefore the lives of the children should be a hostage to public sentiment of the teachings of so beautiful a Mother.

If these pages are of any assistance in preventing mistakes, securing the observance of the conduct proper on special occasions, or causing more consideration for others, their mission will have been fulfilled.

Clergymen have often spoken of the ignorance and thoughtlessness, of the blunders, ludicrous and annoying when not serious, encountered in their parochial work, and this led to the preparation of the little volume which it is hoped, in the conventional phrase, on which the copyright has long since expired, will "fill a long-felt want."

L. H. B.
Easter Monday, March 30, 1891.

For Baptism

It is the Correct Thing

To begin this little book with Baptism, for that is usually the first important event in the life of every Christian.

For parents to have their children baptized as soon as possible, especially if the infant is delicate and seems in danger of death.

For any person, man, woman, or child to baptize a baby in danger of death where the priest cannot be had, or to baptize an adult if he has the proper dispositions, under the same circumstances.

To use only pure water in baptism, pouring it on the head, at the same time pronouncing the words of baptism.

To know that a person is not baptized if the water does not touch the skin.

To have a child baptized in the parish church.

To present it at the time set apart for administering this Sacrament, generally after Mass on weekdays, after Mass or before, and after Vespers on Sundays.

To have not more than two sponsors, a godfather and a godmother, nor less than one.

To have the sponsor of the same sex as the child if there be only one.

To have someone stand for the child by proxy if the sponsor desired cannot be present.

To know that monks and nuns cannot be sponsors.

To know that the priest who baptizes may be the sponsor, provided someone else holds the child and gives the answers.

To invite only practical Catholics to stand for a child, and thus avoid the mortification of having the priest refuse to accept a non-Catholic.

To mention if the child received private baptism.

For the sponsor, or the one presenting the child at the font, to speak the name distinctly and thus avoid a repetition or a mistake.

To hold the child with the head resting on the right arm of the sponsor.

For parents to select at least one name of a saint for the child.

To have the good sense not to expect the priest to baptize a child by a nickname, as Puss, Birdie, or Flossy, or a pagan name, such as Homer or Socrates. Or by a family name alone, as Walsingham Gargery.

To have the clothing about the neck of the child loose, so that the priest may easily anoint the breast and back.

For the sponsor to present an honorarium to the officiating clergyman.

For the father to do likewise if he feels able.

For sponsors to make a present to their godchild, expensive or trifling, as their purse or inclination may dictate.

For sponsors to know that they are obliged in conscience to look after the religious requirements of the child, if it is in danger of not being properly instructed.

To have a christening dinner if the parents wish to do so, to which may be invited the parish priest and the sponsors, and such intimate friends as are desired.

To dress the girls in white and blue, and boys in brown during the first seven years of their lives, to show that they are consecrated to the Blessed Virgin.

To put a little medal or some other sign of Christianity around the child's neck, and always keep it there.[1]

For sponsors to answer the responses clearly and with sincerity.

To repeat audibly the *Apostles' Creed* and the *Our Father* when required to do so by the priest.

For sponsors to place their right hands upon the child at the pouring of the water in the act of baptizing.

To hold the candlestick when the priest presents it.

To remain after baptism until the record, with correct names, is made by the priest.

To have the written permission of the rector, if some grave reason

---

1   Please remember that anything with parts smaller than 1¼ inches around or 2¼ inches long are considered a choking hazard.

impels one to have his child baptized outside of the parish.

To remember, apart from necessity, the parish priest or the one he delegates is the proper person to administer the sacraments to his parishioners.

To remember that parents should not baptize their own children except in danger of death, when no one else is near.

To know that solemn baptism should not be administered in a private house convenient to a church.

For a mother to receive the blessing of the church after childbirth (the ceremony is called *churching*).[2]

To apply at the time appointed by the rector of the church.

To bring a wax candle for use during the blessing.

To make a contribution to the altar if a candle be supplied by the church.

To kneel and hold the lighted candle in the left hand.

To take with the right hand the end of the stole when presented by the priest.

To remain some time in thanksgiving after being sprinkled with holy water.

To always have a Mass offered by way of thanksgiving.

It is Not the Correct Thing

To delay baptism; such neglect may become a grievous sin.

For a parent to baptize his own child, another person being

---

2   *Churching* is a blessing given to mothers, traditionally 40-days after childbirth, to thank God for a safe delivery, and to obtain the graces necessary to bring up her child in a Christian manner. This pious custom dates from the early Christian ages. The prayer is found in the *Rituale Romanum*, and is to be done in a church.

accessible.

For a christening party to present itself at the church when the priests are at dinner, or taking well-earned recreation.

To ask, except in case of necessity, anyone who is not an intimate friend to stand for the child.

To think more of the worldly position than of the piety of the sponsors.

To cherish any hopes that the godparents may leave their godchild a legacy; that happens in story books but rarely in real life, unless the sponsor be a relative.

To have the child so muffled that its head cannot be readily uncovered at the baptismal font.

For the one presenting the child at the font to hold it in such a position that it is uncomfortable, or to frighten it in any way, and thus give it an excuse for trying its vocal chords, to the annoyance of the priest and the confusion of all concerned.

To fail to have it warmly clothed, or to expose it through carelessness or ignorance to any danger of catching cold whilst undergoing the rite of becoming a Christian.

To ask the officiating clergyman how much he charges for baptizing the child. (No charge is ever made for the administration of the sacraments; custom demands an honorarium in proportion to the means of the ones concerned.)

For the father to partake too freely of the flowing bowl in testimony of his joy at the addition to his family.

To bring a non-Catholic or Freemason as sponsor.

To titter and giggle at the antics of the child, or pass remarks.

To make the milk-bottle an intrusive part of the ceremony.

To neglect to wrap up the child before leaving the church, when the weather is severe.

To bring a proxy for a sponsor whose consent was not asked.

For a mother to put off being Churched too long.

To apply to be Churched before the baptism of the child.

To neglect providing a wax candle or a suitable offering.

To hold the candle and stole with the same hand — often costly stoles are ruined by carelessness of this kind.

To pay insufficient attention or to have but little devotion during the blessing.

2

The Correct Thing

At Confession

It is the Correct Thing

For parents to have their children go to confession as soon as they reach the age of reason, generally considered to be when they reach their seventh year.

For parents or teachers to assist their children in the examination of their conscience for their first confession.

To have children go to confession every three months until they make their first Communion.[3]

For adults to go to confession once a month at least, and oftener if advised to do so.

---

3   Since one of the requirements for a Plenary Indulgence is to have gone to Confession within several days (about 20) before or after the indulgenced act, going to Confession every two weeks prepares you soul for a Plenary Indulgence at any time.

For women and children and those who are not employed during the day to go to confession in the afternoon, and leave the evenings and the hour just before supper for men and women who must work for their living.

To examine the conscience well and with scrupulous thoroughness before going into the confessional, and thus avoid unnecessary delay.

For a penitent to take his proper turn in going into the confessional, and not to try to get in ahead of someone else.

To courteously ask the one ahead for his turn if it is absolutely impossible to wait.

For a woman of leisure and piety to offer her turn to a man in a hurry, or a working-woman whose time is precious.

To reserve all matters extraneous from present sins about which one may want the advice of the priest for some other time than Saturday evening, when the confessional is surrounded by weary waiting sinners.

To speak in a whisper, but distinctly, in a tone audible to the confessor but not to those kneeling around the confessional.

To recite the *Confiteor* before going into the confessional, if time is a consideration.

To begin with the formula, "Father, bless me, for I have sinned. Since my last confession which was one month ago" (or one week, two weeks, as the case may be), "I have" — then follow the sins.

To tell the number of times a sin has been committed, also any circumstance that would add to its gravity, so as to save all need of questionings on the part of the priest.

To go up to the front of the church to say one's penance and other prayers, so as to be out of the way of the waiting penitents.

It is Not the Correct Thing

To go into the confessional without having duly examined one's conscience and made all necessary preparation.

To omit to state whether the penance imposed at the last confession was complied with and communion received.

To speak in a tone so loud that those kneeling near the confessional are liable to overhear the confession.

To speak so low and muffled that the priest has to ask for a repetition.

To confess other people's sins, or to mention people's names.

To be unduly scrupulous.

To be careless and mechanical in making one's confession.

To leave the confessional before being dismissed by the priest.

To omit the act of contrition or to say it carelessly.

To fail to ask the confessor to repeat the penance if not understood.

To change confessors too often.

To select a time for a general confession when the church is crowded with weary penitents.

To try to rush in ahead of those kneeling around the confessional and awaiting their turn.

To crowd up too near the confessional.

To ignore the regulation which requires men to enter on one side and women on the other.

To leave the church before making a thanksgiving and saying the penance enjoined, if time will possibly permit of fulfilling that duty.

To tell anyone what penance the priest imposed.

To ask a friend or anyone what penance he received.

3

The Correct Thing

At Holy Communion

It is the Correct Thing

To prepare for Holy Communion by making a good confession, and by fasting from the midnight previous.

To be recollected and to avoid useless conversation before going to the church, and on the way thither.

To spend some time before Mass begins in preparatory devotions.

To be dressed neatly and with scrupulous regard for cleanliness.

For ladies to lift the veil and to remove the gloves before going up to the communion railing.

To walk up to the railing quietly, making as little noise as possible, with the hands clasped upon the breast and eyes cast piously down.

To go up to the railing after the *Domine nonsum dignus*, when the bell rings three times.

To kneel in readiness near the front, if the railing is already filled.

To make the sign of the cross devoutly as the priest pronounces the absolution.

To hold the communion-cloth securely, with both hands under the chin, to raise the head and extend the tongue when the priest approaches with the Sacred Host.

To lower the head after receiving and reverently swallow the Sacred Host.

To leave the railing almost immediately and in concert with those nearest, if there are others waiting to approach the holy table.

To remain at the railing until the tabernacle is closed, if there be only a few communicants.

To remain recollected and in fervent prayer until the end of Mass, before using the prayer book.

To spend some time, at least a quarter of an hour and longer if possible, after Mass in thanksgiving.

To have a regular time for approaching Holy Communion, the first Friday of the month in honor of the Sacred Heart, a certain Sunday of the month, every fortnight, or every week, as conscience or the confessor decides, and to be scrupulous in performing this duty.[4]

To be thoroughly familiar with the scriptural proofs and injunctions in regard to Holy Communion and the teaching of the Church, so as to be ready and willing at all times to give a satisfactory and lucid

---

4   In 1905, Pope St. Pius X declared in SACRA TRIDENTINA (*On Frequent and Daily Reception of Holy Communion*) that frequent and daily Communion should be open to all the faithful.

explanation to non-Catholics.

To know that the smallest quantity of food breaks the fast.

To know that to swallow the saliva does not break the fast.

To cleanse the mouth and teeth the evening before Communion.

To remember that the fast is not required when Holy Communion is received as a viaticum.

To remember that one may offer his Holy Communion for any special intention, for a friend, for our Holy Father, superiors, relatives, the conversion of sinners, or the suffering souls in Purgatory.

To not forget one's own special needs.

To know that the tenth is the day for receiving Holy Communion after making a novena.

To know that every Catholic is bound to receive Holy Communion within the Easter-time. In the United States this precept obliges from the first Sunday in Lent to Trinity Sunday inclusive.

To know that the paschal Communion should be received in one's own parish church.

To know that one confined to his house by sickness is still obliged to receive Holy Communion there if he finds it impossible to go to the church.

To notify the parish priest when aged or infirm persons are not able to approach Holy Communion in the church.

For both parents and children to approach Holy Communion at times together.

It is Not the Correct Thing

To go to a party or to the theatre the evening before approaching Holy Communion.

To laugh and talk needlessly on the way to church.

To omit making a preparation before Mass begins.

To wear torn or soiled apparel.[5]

To have paint or powder on the face or eyebrows.[6]

To have soiled hands and long, dirty fingernails.

To stalk heavily up to the railing, the arms at the side, the eyes wandering around the church.

To go up to the railing before the proper time.

To wait until everybody is already at the railing and then go marching up, causing useless disturbance.

To try to crowd in when the railing is already full, instead of waiting patiently for the next round.

To wait until the priest has already started up the altar-steps, thinking that there are no more communicants, and then to go up to the railing, causing needless delay.

To hold the communion-cloth so carelessly that if a particle of the Sacred Host were to fall from the lips it would be in danger of dropping off the cloth.

To hold the head down so low that the priest has trouble in conveying the Sacred Host to the tongue.

---

5 When nicer clothing is available to you.

6 Garish make-up. St. Thomas Aquinas said this about women using cosmetics: "...such painting does not always involve a mortal sin, but only when it is done for the sake of sensuous pleasure or in contempt of God."

To remain kneeling at the railing when others are waiting to approach.

To walk hurriedly back to the seat with the hands unclasped and the eyes not cast down.

To clasp the hands with the fingers pointing downward.

To rush out of church as soon as Mass is over without making any thanksgiving.

To expectorate shortly after receiving.

To have no regular time for approaching the Sacraments of penance and the Holy Eucharist.

To go but once a year, or even every few months.

To give vague, and worse still, erroneous explanations in regard to the Holy Eucharist when questioned by non-Catholics.

4

The Correct Thing

For Confirmation

It is the Correct Thing

For children to be confirmed at the first opportunity after they have made their first Communion.

For adults who neglected to receive this sacrament in their youth to do so at the first chance offered. Those who neglect are guilty of grievous sin.

To prepare for the reception of this sacrament by a good confession, as the Holy Ghost will not enter a soul defiled with sin.

For young girls to wear white, and the boys neat new suits.

To study carefully beforehand the ceremonies and symbols used in the administration of this sacrament.

To know that this sacrament can be received only once, and that a person would commit a sacrilege if he attempted to receive it a second time. And that it would also be a sacrilege to receive it in mortal sin.

To take the name of one's favorite saint for a confirmation name.

It is Not the Correct Thing

For parents to neglect to have their children confirmed after they have made their first Communion.

For adults who have had no opportunity to receive the sacrament of confirmation in youth to continue to live without its grace.

To receive this sacrament carelessly and in ignorance of its meaning.

To omit a contribution in proportion to one's means towards defraying the expense attendant upon the administration of this sacrament.

To be confirmed with the baptismal name.

To omit sponsors at confirmation.

To forget that sponsors for confirmation, like godparents at baptism, are related by spiritual affinity to their godchildren as well as the parents of their godchildren; hence godparents cannot marry godchildren or the parents of their godchildren, yet one godparent may marry the other.

5

The Correct Thing
For the Sick

It is the Correct Thing

To send for the parish priest as soon as a person becomes dangerously ill.

For the sick person, if not in imminent danger of death, to make his confession during the first visit of the priest, and to wait for a second visit for the Holy Communion.

For the nurse or some member of the patient's family to place a chair for the priest by the side of the bed, raise the patient to a comfortable posture, inquire of the priest if he desires anything, and then withdraw whilst the confession is being heard.

To keep everybody from intruding in the sickroom whilst the priest is hearing the confession and giving spiritual consolation.

When the priest is expected with the Holy Communion, to have the room put in order and everything made ready.

To have a table prepared, covered with a clean white cloth, and upon it at least one candlestick holding a blessed wax candle lighted, a crucifix, two small glasses, one containing holy water and the other pure fresh water (for the ablution after Communion), pure cotton balls, and a tablespoon.

For some one holding a lighted candle to meet the priest at the door when he arrives with the Blessed Sacrament, and to precede him to the place prepared.

For all in the room to kneel when the priest enters with the Sacred Host.

After the priest has sprinkled the bed with holy water, repeated the antiphon, "*Asperges me*, Thou shalt sprinkle me," etc., and said the prayer, "*Exaudi nos, Domine*" for an attendant to recite the *Confiteor*, if the patient is too weak to do so.

To have the hair combed, the face washed, the mouth rinsed out, and the bed of the sick person made tidy before the priest arrives.

For one who suffers a prolonged illness to receive Holy Communion frequently, even though not in danger of death.

To know that the receiving of Holy Communion, even as Viaticum, will not hasten death.

To know that a sick person need not be fasting in order to receive the Holy Viaticum.

For a person who is dangerously ill to attend to all worldly matters the first thing, so that there will be nothing to distract the mind from spiritual concerns.

To receive *Extreme Unction* whilst the patient still has the use of his senses.

To sponge off the parts to be anointed — the eyes, the ears, the nostrils, the mouth, the hands, the feet — before the arrival of the priest.

To know that *Extreme Unction* can be received only once in the same sickness, unless there is a partial recovery and then a serious relapse, in which case it may be received again.

To know that only those in danger of death by sickness can receive this sacrament; that soldiers going to battle, persons in a storm at sea, criminals about to be executed, cannot receive *Extreme Unction*.

To know, however, that soldiers who have been wounded, persons dying from an accident, those washed ashore in whom life is not yet extinct, can and should be anointed.

To know that infants and those born with severe mental deficiencies cannot be anointed, since they cannot commit sin.

To know that those dying impenitent, or in a state of mortal sin — as a drunkard in his drunkenness — or in the commission of a crime — as a man shot in a duel — cannot receive this sacrament unless there is some reason to think that at the moment of death there is sincere penitence.

For all present at the administration of the last sacraments to join in the prayers for the dying.

If the patient be a woman, for another woman to make the sign of the cross upon her forehead, mouth, and breast, if she is unable to do so herself at the proper time in the prayers for the dying.

For a patient to accept the illness as coming from God, and to bear the suffering in union with the sufferings and death of Our Lord.

To be patient and resigned. To take the medicine and nourishment prescribed.

To have a crucifix, a Rosary, and some holy water constantly within reach.

For relatives and friends to be as calm and composed as possible. To exclude all worldly considerations from the chamber of the dying.

For some one of those in attendance on a dying person to keep reciting suitable prayers until the soul has left the body.

To have one or more blessed candles lighted near the bedside.

To press the crucifix to the dying lips and to sprinkle the bed repeatedly with holy water.

To know that candles are blessed in all churches on Candlemas day, and that every Catholic should provide himself with some.

To know that the candles should be wax.

To know that all members of a parish, whether they go to the parish church or not, can only be attended in case of sickness by the priests belonging to the parish, unless in special cases permission is obtained from the parish rector to have a priest from another parish who may have been the confessor or the life-long friend of the person who is ill.

To always provide a companion or attendant when sending for a priest after dark.

To insist upon seeing the priest back home to his own house.

To abstain from conversation if the priest is carrying the Blessed Sacrament, and to accompany with prayer.

In country places where the priest lives a great distance and his call entails expense, to cover the amount not with thanks alone, but with means to pay railroad fare or horse hire.

It is Not the Correct Thing

To defer sending for the priest until death is imminent and the patient almost speechless.

To go for the priest in the middle of the night when the patient is not in danger of dying without the sacraments.

To omit having the table with the candle, etc., prepared when the priest is expected with the Sacred Host.

To use a dingy or colored cover, a broken spoon, a dirty glass for the water, or a candle that has not been blessed.

To be without holy water.* (*Holy water is blessed every Sunday before the High Mass and may be obtained by anyone providing a clean bottle. Ask the serving boy, or if there is a pail for the convenience of the people, help yourself.)

To have no crucifix in the house.

To forget to light the candles.

To allow anyone in the room who will not act with proper respect whilst the priest is administering the sacraments.

To alarm the patient with exaggerated accounts of his illness.

To deceive the patient with false assurances as to his condition.

To oppose sending for the priest if the patient desires his presence, whether he is in danger of death or not.

To omit telling the priest when a visit of consolation merely is desired, so that he can choose his own time for paying the call.

To omit informing the priest when any member of a family is ill.

To go for a priest outside of the parish, as a priest is not supposed to answer sick-calls outside of his own parish.[7]

To allow whispering, needless talking, or strong outbursts of grief in the sick-room whilst the priest is administering the sacraments.

To omit saying the prayers for the dying if the priest can not be had.

To be careless, etc., in complying with the last requests of the dying.

---

7   Common sense indicates that, in case of necessity, any priest will be more than happy to fulfill his priestly vocation of availing the sacraments to all.

The Correct Thing
For a Funeral

It is the Correct Thing

For the relatives and nearest friends of the deceased to have Masses said as soon as possible for the repose of his soul.

To have the funeral conducted from the parish church.

To have a Requiem Mass celebrated on the day of the funeral.

To place a crucifix on the lifeless breast in the coffin.

To keep blessed candles constantly burning around the remains.

To refuse admission to all callers save relatives and very dear friends.

For a Catholic to be buried in a Catholic cemetery, or at least in a consecrated grave.

To pay church expenses connected with a funeral in advance.

It is Not the Correct Thing

For relatives and friends to spend a great deal of money for flowers and the trappings of woe and little or none for Masses.

For those in attendance at a "wake" to make it the occasion of merriment.

For people who are not rich to have a great many carriages.

For friends who cannot afford the expense to send expensive floral offerings.

To have a Protestant minister hold any kind of funeral services over the body of a Catholic in deference to the feelings of his Protestant relatives.

For friends to spend money for a carriage and for flowers and neglect to have a Mass offered up for the departed soul.

To make a vulgar display of a profusion of flowers and a long line of carriages.

To expect a consecrated grave and a priest to conduct funeral service for one who refused the ministrations of the Church whilst living.

For friends to be careless and neglectful about attending the funeral and offering the consolation of sympathy and any little service in their power to the bereaved family.

For mere acquaintances and strangers to crowd the church through a morbid curiosity, and to attempt to get front seats which belong by all courtesy and right to the mourners.

And worse still, for them to take advantage of so sad an occasion to get a free drive, and occupy carriages provided for relatives and friends.

To speak of the faults of the dead.

7

The Correct Thing
In Marriage Engagements

It is the Correct Thing

For a young lady to think well about what she is doing before engaging herself in marriage.

For a young man to ponder seriously the same subject.

As a general rule, for Catholics to marry Catholics.

In case that one of the parties to a marriage engagement is a Protestant, to ascertain that there will be no trouble in obtaining all the promises required by the Church from the non-Catholic before announcing the engagement.

To ascertain in all cases where a dispensation is required whether it can be procured without any difficulty before announcing an engagement.

To know that a dispensation is required for Catholics to marry non-Catholics, cousins within and including the fourth degree; persons related by marriage within the fourth degree; persons connected by spiritual affinity — sponsors, god-children, etc.

To know that dispensations are not mere matters of form, and that they will not be given unless there are grave reasons for doing so.

To know that a tax for some charitable object must be given when obtaining a dispensation.

To give timely notice of an engagement to the parish priest, so that the banns may be published three successive Sundays.

To consult parents, or other persons of sound judgment, and the pastor, before entering into an engagement of marriage.

To remember that both head and heart should agree in the choice of a companion for life.

For a rich young man to give his fiancée a handsome diamond solitaire engagement-ring.

For one who is poor to select an inexpensive ring in keeping with his means, and save his money for the more necessary needs of house-keeping.

For a prospective bride in the preparation of her *trousseau* to patronize orphan industrial institutions, religious communities who make a specialty of this kind of work, and needy and deserving seamstresses, in preference to those who are merely fashionable.

To insist on having a quiet wedding if the parents cannot afford the expense of an elaborate one.

For a prospective bride to make a religious retreat in a convent, or wherever it is most convenient, before her wedding-day. A like exercise would be very beneficial for the groom.

To have the banns proclaimed on three successive Sundays in the parishes of both the contracting parties.

For an engaged couple to avoid public displays of affection, which are both vulgar and indiscreet.

It is Not the Correct Thing

To enter into an engagement without due deliberation.

To enter into an engagement merely for amusement, as an outcome of a summer's acquaintance, and with no intention of fulfilling it by marriage. Such a course is not only un-Christian, but decidedly ill-bred; and a young lady who is guilty of such an impropriety brings down upon herself the severest strictures of society.

To receive marked attentions from a stranger whose antecedents and past conduct are not perfectly well known.

For a young lady to permit serious and exclusive attentions from a gentleman whom she has no thought of marrying.

To receive expensive presents from a gentleman. Both social usage and womanly instinct forbid this.

To go out driving alone with a gentleman.

To marry a man simply because he is rich.

To enter into an engagement without the consent and approval of parents or guardians.

To let parents persuade one into a marriage of convenience where there is no congeniality.

To think more of the worldly advantages than of the spiritual effects of a marriage.

To give up all the time of an engagement to amusement and none to religious duties.

For a bride to have her *trousseau* made where she can have it done the cheapest, with no thought to the suffering of underpaid seamstresses. If she wishes a blessing stitched in with the dainty laces, she will try to make her wedding an occasion of benefit to the poor, and to all who have anything to do with it.

To insist on a costly wedding where the parents cannot afford it.

To seek to have the proclamation of the banns dispensed with unless there is an especial reason for doing so.

To blame the priest because marriage is delayed through ignorance of the contracting parties or neglect in giving timely notice.

8

The Correct Thing
For a Wedding

It is the Correct Thing

To be married in the parish church.

To be married in the morning at a nuptial Mass.

For the bride and bridegroom to approach Holy Communion on their wedding day.

For their parents and near relatives to do the same thing.

For the bridal cortège to be on time and not keep the clergyman and guests waiting.

To remember that by receiving the sacrament of matrimony in a state of mortal sin one commits a sacrilege, and forfeits all the graces attached to its worthy reception.

To remember that Lent and Advent are prohibited times for solemnizing marriage.

To defray promptly all expenses connected with a wedding, such as lights, decorations, music, etc.

For a bridegroom, through his best man, to present the officiating clergyman with a sum in proportion to his means and his joy at winning a bride. Ten dollars is considered a decent honorary, which may be increased according to means.

If the wedding is in the evening, for the bride, bridesmaids, and invited guests to be properly attired. (Evening weddings are generally forbidden by the Bishops, hence they are not usual now.)

For the guests to remember that talking and whispering are as much out of place at a church wedding as such conduct would be at any other time in the presence of the Blessed Sacrament.

For the bride to omit gloves.

For the bridegroom to have the ring placed upon the plate.

To present the license where the law requires such.

To have at least two witnesses.

To give the proper names of the contracting parties.

To join hands whilst reciting the marriage formula.

To kneel in the sanctuary if place be provided.

For attendants and witnesses to kneel in the front pews.

To kneel at the lowest altar-step at the *Pater Noster*, when assisting at the nuptial Mass.

To receive Holy Communion at the *prie dieu*.

To approach the altar-step before the blessing.

If the rector have other arrangements than the above, to follow them.

For the people of a parish to remember that a wedding is a private affair, and that only those invited are expected to attend.

To make a wedding an occasion of joy to the relatives and friends of the contracting parties, and also to the poor.

To have an elegant and costly reception if one's means permit.

For a bride to be dignified, affable, modest, and winning at her bridal reception.

It is Not the Correct Thing

To want to be married in other than the parish church simply because it may not be a fashionable or costly structure.

To omit the nuptial Mass without some grave reason.

To be married in the evening if it can be avoided.

To require expensive decorations in the church without advancing the means to pay for them.

To make any arrangement about organist, singers, or music, without consulting the rector of the church beforehand.

To introduce favorite secular songs or secularized religious music into the service. This is exceedingly bad form. All attraction in a Catholic church is at the altar, not in the choir-loft.

For the bride and groom to come to the church unaccompanied.

To come late, to forget the ring or license.

To neglect a suitable honorary for the officiating clergyman.

To endeavor to introduce unusual or un-Catholic ceremonies in the church.

To fail in procuring the necessary dispensation in cases of mixed marriages (a Catholic with a non-Catholic).

To give any but the true family name, even when a person for some reason may be known by another.

To begin congratulations before the parties have left the church.

To forget that the late council of Baltimore prohibited the celebration of weddings in church after five o'clock in the evening.

To omit going to confession and Communion before receiving the sacrament of marriage.

To ask for a dispensation as to the prohibited times of marriage without some exceedingly grave reason. A wedding should be a time of joy, and is therefore out of place in a season of preparation and penance. In case a dispensation is granted the marriage must be private.

To be a penny-pincher in feeing the clergyman. Clergymen make a practice of accepting nothing from those in poverty.

For a woman to enter the church in a décolleté gown.

For bridesmaids or guests to go into the presence of the Blessed Sacrament without a covering on their heads.

To laugh, talk, or whisper in church.

For those not invited to seek to enter a church at a wedding, as if it were a mere show.

To spend more than can be well afforded on wedding festivities.

For those invited who cannot afford the expense to send costly presents.

For a bride to be giddy at her wedding reception.

For guests to manifest their good feeling by imbibing too freely of the wines provided. It is very easy for a man to drink more than he can stand at a wedding banquet, and yet there is no conduct more ungentlemanly and more annoying to the hostess.

To omit an invitation to the reception to the officiating clergyman and the priests of the parish.

The Correct Thing
In Church

It is the Correct Thing

To always be in time for Mass and other services in the church.

To remember that the church-bells are rung for a purpose and not merely to keep the sexton busy, and that it would be well therefore to obey their call.[8]

For every member of a parish to rent a pew or at least a seat in the parish church.[9]

To take holy water upon entering the church.

To make the sign of the cross on the person and not in the air.

---

8 The church-bells were rung three times a day, at 6:00 A.M., 12:00 P.M. and 6:00 P.M., summoning the faithful to pray the *Angelus*.

9 Until the turn of century, a common method of tithing in Anglican, Catholic, and Presbyterian churches was to rent pews to families or individuals.

To genuflect on the right knee and to have it touch the floor.

To remember that the King of kings is present on the altar, and to order one's conduct accordingly.

To avoid whispering, laughing, and looking about in church.

To walk gently up the aisle if one is unavoidably detained until after the services have begun.

To make a short act of adoration on bended knees after entering the pew.

To be devout and recollected at the different parts of the Mass.

To remember that mere bodily presence in the church with the mind wandering to temporal concerns, does not fulfill the precept of hearing Mass.

To pay attention to the sermon, and make it the subject of one's thoughts during the day, as also during the week.

To remember when special collections are to be taken up, and to have a contribution ready in your hand.

To make a practice of putting something in the contribution-box every Sunday. To train children to this practice.

To listen to the music as a means of elevating the heart to God.

For a gentleman occupying a pew to move in or rise and let ladies pass in before him.

For pew-holders to offer seats in their pews to strangers.

To seat non-Catholics rather away from the altar. Experience teaches that they often forget their manners.

For men too stingy to have seats of their own in church to occupy the free pews, and not blockade the entrance by standing, or kneeling on one knee, around it.

To avoid coughing, moving the feet around, or making any noise to the annoyance of clergy and people.

To leave babies at home or with a neighbor when going to church.

For a mother who has her child with her at church to get up and take it out when it begins to cry or fret.

To be punctilious in following the ceremonials of the church, standing, kneeling, etc., at the proper times.

For non-Catholics who go to Catholic churches to conform to the services, and to remember that this is a requirement of good breeding.

For Catholics to keep away from Protestant services. It is strictly prohibited to acknowledge heretical worship or assent to heretical doctrine.

For members of the choir to sing for the glory of God and not for their own.

To take an earnest Protestant to hear a good sermon.

To remain kneeling until the last prayers have been said and the priest has retired to the sacristy.

It is Not the Correct Thing

To be late for Mass or any church service.

To stalk hurriedly and noisily up the aisle

To ignore the holy water font at the entrance.

To make the sign of the cross as if fanning off flies.

To give a little bobbing curtsy, instead of the proper genuflection, before entering one's pew.

To whisper, laugh, or cause any distraction to those around.

To deliberately turn around, stare up at the choir, or at those entering the church.

To go to sleep, or read the prayer-book during the sermon. (This is unpardonable.)

To be in an ecstatic condition of devotion when the contribution-box approaches.

To forget all about the special collections for the orphans, the church debt, the pope, etc.

To go to High Mass simply to listen to the music as one would go to the opera.

For a person occupying the end seat to scowl forbiddingly at all those who seek to enter the pew.

For a person to go to a private pew without an invitation.

To take babies or sick and crying children to church.

To make a rush for the door before the priest has even descended the altar to begin the concluding prayers.

To go to church at the last moment and to leave it at the first.

To take non-Catholics to Mass who will not behave themselves as the presence of the Blessed Sacrament demands. When the question of offence is between God and man, there should be no hesitation in deciding.

To kneel on only one knee, or to emulate the position of the bear when saying one's prayers.

For members of the choir to forget that the choir-loft is a part of the church, and that talking, laughing, giggling, chewing gum, and other practices which have been known to prevail in some choirs are strictly out of place. It has been remarked that in choir conduct Catholic members, to their shame, suffer in comparison with Protestants.

For members of the congregation to find fault with the sermon, criticize the clergyman, and retail gossip on their way home from church, as is done in China and other places in the Orient.

The Correct Thing

At High Mass

It is the Correct Thing

To be in time. To stand at the *Asperges me.*[10] To make the sign of the cross when sprinkled.

To kneel until the *Gloria.*

To rise and remain standing whilst this hymn is being recited by the celebrant.

To sit whilst it is being sung by the choir.

To sit whilst the celebrant sits.

To rise with the celebrant and remain standing until the chanting of the Epistle.

---

10   Some of these refer to the details of the Tridentine Latin Mass, also more recently known as the Extraordinary Form. However, the sentiments remain the same.

To sit from the beginning of the Epistle to the Gospel.

To remain standing during the singing of the Gospel.

To make the sign of the cross on forehead, lips, and breast.

To kneel if the *Veni Creator* is sung before the sermon.

To sit until the reading of the Gospel by the preacher.

To stand while the preacher reads the Gospel in the vernacular.

To sit still and listen attentively to the word of God.

To stand whilst the *Credo* is being said by the celebrant.

To sit while it is sung by the choir.

To stand at the *Dominus Vobiscum* and *Oremus*.

To sit or kneel at the Offertory.

To stand whilst being incensed at a solemn High Mass.

To stand at the singing of the Preface and the *Pater Noster*.

To kneel at the *Sanctus* and remain on the knees until after the first ablution.

To stand at the Orations and until the singing of the *Ite Missa est*.

To devoutly receive the blessing kneeling, and to bless one's self.

To stand at the Gospel, making the sign of the cross on forehead, lips, and breast.

To leave babbling babies at home. [Write this deep in the memory.]

To remain in one's seat until after the priest has left the sanctuary.

To remember that the church vestibule is not a reception-room for the interchange of friendly greetings and current gossip.

It is Not the Correct Thing

To march up the aisle to a front pew if one enters the church after Mass has begun.

To whisper in church or to nod to acquaintances.

To stand, sit, or kneel, just as it suits one's fancy to do, without any regard to the services.

To turn in one's seat and stare up at the choir, or spread out the arms on the back of the pew.

To go to church to learn the latest fashions.

To fail to take along a prayer-book or Rosary.

To impede the exit from the church by standing to talk to one's friends.

For men and boys to loiter around the church entrance, staring at passers-by.

For those occupying pews near the altar to attempt to leave the church first.

To omit to take holy water at the church door on leaving, or to converse while leaving.

To fail to remain for a meeting or conference called by the rector.

To remain seated and to stare at the people as they pass out.

To leave the church as if exhausted and glad to get out. [A little meditation might inform such a person that he does not know what he is doing — is ignorant of the doctrines of his Church, or the state of his interior requires considerable repairing.]

The Correct Thing
For Lent

It is the Correct Thing

To begin the holy and penitential season of Lent by assisting at Mass and partaking of the blessed ashes on Ash Wednesday.[11]

To resolve to observe all the regulations of the church as far as one is able.

To abstain from all worldly amusements from motives of piety and not because it is bad form to keep up social dissipations during Lent. Society closes its doors during this time.

To decline all invitations to amusements.

To remember that a woman who is able to keep up the round of social enjoyments all winter ought to be able to fast during Lent.

---

11   Many of the Lenten practices listed in this chapter have been "lessened" by Holy Mother Church.

To be punctilious about attending the Lenten devotions Sundays, Wednesdays, and Fridays.

To assist at the daily Mass if at all possible.

To take but one full meal on any day in Lent (Sundays excepted), and then not till after twelve o'clock.

To know that when it is the custom to take dinner in the evening and not at midday, a collation is permitted in the morning.

To know that fish (oysters) and meat cannot be used at the same meal during any day in Lent, even on Sundays.

To know that meat is allowed but once a day except on Sundays.

To know that on Wednesdays and Fridays meat is not allowed, nor is it allowed on the second Saturday in Lent (Ember-day) or Holy Saturday. That if the dinner or full meal is taken at noon, one may take a cup of tea, coffee, or thin chocolate in the morning, and a collation, which is about the one-fourth of any ordinary meal, in the evening.

To know that one is obliged to fast as soon as he finishes his twenty-first year, or begins his twenty-second.

That children should abstain from meat when they reach the age of seven years.

To remember that abstinence and fasting are two different things.

Every Friday in the year is a day of abstinence but is not a fast-day.

Every day in Lent except Sundays is a fast-day.

To remember that sick, convalescent, or delicate people are not obliged to fast. That those engaged at hard labor, tradesmen generally, railroaders, steamboat-men, etc., are not obliged to fast.

To know that every Saturday in the year is a day of abstinence like Friday, but the people in the United States are exempt at the present time.

To lay aside the pipe or the bottle during Lent.

To devote the time of Lent to a building up of one's spiritual life.

To make Lent a red-letter period for the poor and suffering.

To remember that travelers should keep Lent abroad as well as at home, and that the mere fact of leaving home does not abrogate the Lenten obligations.

It is Not the Correct Thing

To begin the Lenten season by grumbling.

To keep Lent because it is fashionable to do so.

To occupy one's time in preparing for the post-Lenten festivities.

To fail to attend the Stations of the Cross, as well as the Wednesday and Sunday evening instructions.

To neglect daily Mass when able to attend. In cities where there are early Masses in nearly all churches, one who wishes, with a little mortification, may attend Mass.

To neglect spiritual reading, religious instructions, and acts of self-denial.

To omit works of charity when the occasion of doing good presents itself.

To begin Lent with the proper dispositions, and relax before it is over.

To neglect works of penance when one is free from the obligations of fasting.

To take milk, thick chocolate, or highly sweetened coffee in the morning.

To take butter, eggs, cake, pie, or anything but a cracker in the morning.

To eat meat at the evening collation.

To be guided by the example of negligent Catholics rather than the written law of the Church.

To discuss the propriety or impropriety of the Lenten regulations, or to find fault with them.

To forget that far from being a pleasure, the Lenten season is a time of penance and should be spent accordingly.

For parents to show a negligence in the observance of Lent, and thus give bad example to their children.

For anyone to dispense himself from the Lenten obligation.

To forget that the pastor is the proper person to dispense.

12

The Correct Thing
During Holy Week

It is the Correct Thing

To redouble one's devotions during Holy Week.

To be on time for all the Holy Week services.

To provide one's self with a Holy Week manual so as to be able to follow the services with intelligence and spiritual profit.

To contribute to the fund for decorating the repository for Holy Thursday in the parish church.

To genuflect on both knees when visiting repositories on Holy Thursday, as is the regulation at all times when the Blessed Sacrament is exposed in a church.

To peremptorily stop all whispering and irreverence on the part of non-Catholic companions who accompany one from motives of curiosity to the different churches.

To remember that one who walks to the different churches visited gains more merit than one who rides, other things being equal.

To receive Holy Communion on Holy Thursday.

To know that a great many indulgences can be obtained by piously attending the Holy Week services.

To go up one aisle and to come down another when visiting repositories in crowded churches, so as to avoid jostling against the throng.

It is Not the Correct Thing

To think that by being pious during Holy Week one can atone for laxity during the other five weeks of Lent.

To straggle into the church after the services have begun.

To gaze around or to whisper during the solemn services.

To sit down where the ritual requires one to kneel or stand.

Through negligence to fail to provide one's self with a Holy Week manual, and thereby for the sake of fifty cents, or to save a little trouble.

To miss the abundant spiritual benefits which accrue from faithfully following the services.

To forget that the beautiful repositories with their wealth of flowers and their dazzling tapers cost money.

To fail to make the proper genuflection upon entering and leaving the church.

To answer the questions of non-Catholic companions whilst in the presence of the Blessed Sacrament.

To turn Holy Thursday into a day of pleasure.

To be so ungrateful for the inestimable blessing of the Blessed Sacrament as to fail to approach the holy table on the day of its institution.

The Correct Thing

At a Religious Reception or Profession

It is the Correct Thing

To solicit an invitation to a religious reception if one has any particular reason for desiring to be present.

For guests to go in time so as to be in their places before the ceremonies begin.

To yield the front seats to the relatives and friends of the novices and candidates.

To let one's conduct be as reverential as it should be at any other time in the presence of the Blessed Sacrament.

To avoid standing up on the seats in order to get a better view of the ceremonies.

To refrain from whispered comments on the appearance of the

brides-elect or the ceremonies.

To be contented to stand if there are no vacant seats.

To congratulate the new religious on their admission into the conventual life.

If there is a particular Sister whom one wishes to see, to go to the parlor and ask for her.

For the parents or guardian of the candidate for the religious life to provide her with a white gown, tulle veil, etc., exactly as for a bride of the world.

For relatives and friends to partake of the collation in convents where it is customary to provide one.

It is Not the Correct Thing

To go to a religious reception to which invitations have been issued, without such invitation.

To forget that it is just as rude to go to a reception at a convent after the ceremonies have begun as it would be to arrive late at a dinner-party.

For strangers to crowd into the front seats, to the annoyance of the relatives and friends who have a right to them.

To talk, laugh, or stare about.

To be offended if an invitation is refused

To forget that convent chapels are usually small and can only contain a limited number of persons.

To go to a reception and then rush off without a word of congratulation to the new religious.

To take advantage of one's admission into the convent precincts to wander around the building and intrude in places forbidden to lay people to enter.

For those who are neither relatives nor friends of the new Sisters to partake of the refreshments provided, unless asked by one of the Sisters to do so.

To partake of the hospitality of the convent and then turn around and criticize one's entertainers.

14

The Correct Thing

When Visiting Convents

It is the Correct Thing

To make one's visits to a convent on the regulation visiting-days.

To show the same good breeding one would in a private house.

To comply with all the regulations in regard to visitors.

If one desires to go through the house, to ask the Superior if it would be convenient to her to grant that privilege.

To let the Sister who is conducting the visitors through the house invariably lead the way.

To pause but a moment in a room where the pupils are assembled, unless invited to remain longer.

To be careful not to disturb the nuns at their devotions nor the children at their studies by loud tones or laughter.

To ask any desired information in a courteous, well-bred way.

To remember that there are some things which are purely private.

To kneel for a moment when taken to the chapel. Christians can avail themselves of the opportunity to say an extra prayer, and advanced thinkers (?) can demonstrate their good breeding by an outward conformance to usage.

To genuflect when passing the chapel door.

To avoid stepping on the polished floors when there is matting spread to protect them.

To refrain from all uncomplimentary comments.

To remember that Sisters are no fonder of fulsome flattery than other people, and no more obtuse in recognizing it.

To show proper appreciation in the studio and the museum.

To listen respectfully to the pious legends and convent annals with which the good Sisters may seek to edify their visitors.

To remember that the poor-boxes found in charitable institutions are not put there for ornament.

To thank the Sister who has conducted one through a convent, and to express the pleasure afforded by the visit.

For parents, relatives, and friends visiting children at school to positively discountenance all tale-bearing.

If there is any fault to be found with the treatment of a pupil either in regard to discipline or class, to ask for the Superior or Directress, and lay the complaint frankly and courteously before her.

To remember that an open complaint will be appreciated much more than secret fault-finding.

To remember that there are two sides to every question.

To act in a convent parlor as one would in a private house.

To encourage pupils to follow the rules and regulations of the institution.

To take for granted that the Superior and her assistants know their business and are not in need of unsolicited instruction.

To provide children with proper wearing apparel.

To remember that a convent is not the place for fashionable attire.

It is Not the Correct Thing

To seek admission into a convent on the class-days, when visitors are not wanted.

To spend the time whilst waiting in walking around the parlor, criticizing the pictures, fingering the ornaments, etc.

To say "we want to go through the house," as if that were a right instead of only a privilege.

To rush ahead of the conductress and into rooms probably not open to visitors.

To spend some time in a classroom disturbing the pupils and taking their minds from their lessons.

To forget that loud laughter and shrill tones are particularly out of place in a convent.

To ask a Sister why she became a nun, where she came from, what her family name was, if she ever wishes she were back in the world, how much dowry is required for entrance, if the novitiate is very strict, if they are allowed enough to eat, if she does not think that convents are behind the times; or to say that the convent would be much nicer if it had the modern improvements; that the Blank Convent is a far more fashionable one; that nuns are only human beings after all; that convents are good institutions for girls to learn their catechism, fancy-work, and penmanship in, and for those who do not care for a higher education; to offer to send a catalogue of Clap Trap College so that the Sisters can cribbage some advanced ideas; to ask why they do not employ professors for music and drawing; to say that one would rather be dead than be a nun, and to express unbounded sympathy for the misguided mortals who were ever persuaded into sacrificing their lives.

To go to the other extreme.

To indulge in rhapsodies over the amateur daubs found in the studio.

To act when in the chapel as if one's knees were made of wood without any joints.

To forget that in a purely charitable institution the clasp of one's purse ought not to be like the mouth of a clam.

To take one's departure without a word of acknowledgment as to the pleasure afforded by the visit.

For parents to encourage their children in finding fault with their teachers or mistresses.

To forget that the Superioress is a lady and entitled to the respect due a lady as well as to her office.

To forget that it is dishonorable to carry tales out of school.

To ask to take pupils out of the convent on any other than the regulation days without exceedingly grave reasons.

For anyone to carry letters or notes, under any circumstances, either in or out of a convent.

To make frequent or unnecessary visits.

15

The Correct Thing
In Regard to Indulgences

It is the Correct Thing

For Catholics to understand thoroughly the nature of indulgences.

To know that an indulgence is the release from the canonical penance enjoined on the penitent in the early days of the Church in punishment for certain sins.

That an indulgence also remits the whole or a part of the temporal punishment due to sin, either here or in Purgatory.

That Christ Himself gave the Church power to grant indulgences when He said to St. Peter, "Whatsoever thou shalt loose upon earth it shall be loosed also in heaven."

That the source of indulgences is in the super-abundant merits of Our Lord, the Blessed Virgin, and the saints.

To know that in former times sinners were required to do penance for a certain length of time, as seven years, ten years, a quarantine, or forty days, a hundred days, etc., and that an indulgence for seven years, etc., means a remission of that penance. [A quarantine means a penance equivalent to a Lent — seven quarantines mean a penance of seven Lents.]

That the Church does not regard sin as less offensive now than formerly, but that she grants indulgences more frequently because she wishes to assist our weakness and to supply our insufficiency in satisfying the divine justice for our transgressions.

That indulgences are divided into two kinds, plenary and partial.

That a plenary indulgence remits all the temporal punishment due to sin.

That a partial indulgence remits only a part of the temporal punishment due to sin.

To know that indulgences are also divided into perpetual indulgences and indulgences for only a limited time; that they are again divided into local, real, and personal indulgences.

Perpetual indulgences are granted without any limitation of time; temporary indulgences are only for a certain time; local indulgences are limited to particular places; personal indulgences are indulgences granted to particular persons.

To know that a person must be in a state of grace before an indulgence can be obtained.

That to gain a plenary indulgence one must be heartily sorry for every sin, and have no affection even for the smallest venial sin.

That to gain an indulgence one must perform all of the works prescribed; and that if unable to fulfill some of the conditions, the indulgence can not be gained without having the conditions commuted by an authorized person into some other good work.

To know that an indulgence is not a pardon for sin either past, present, or future, but of the temporal punishment due to past sin, after the sin is forgiven in the Sacrament of Penance

To know that indulgences have never been either bought or sold, historians (?) to the contrary.

To know that an indulgence cannot be gained without a sincere sorrow for sin, and therefore it could not by any possibility be a license to commit sin.

That the usual conditions for gaining an indulgence are confession, Communion joined with the other good works, and prayers prescribed by the Church.

To know that indulgences cannot be applied to the souls in Purgatory unless so declared.

That it is more meritorious to apply indulgences to the poor souls than to one's self.

It is Not the Correct Thing

To imagine, as some Catholics do, that an indulgence is the remission of a certain length of time which would otherwise have to be spent in Purgatory.

That it is a remission of the punishment due to all the sins committed during the seven or ten years, or whatever the time may be, specified in the indulgence.

To believe that popes ever sold indulgences.

To think that one can gain an indulgence whilst in the state of mortal sin, or a plenary indulgence when one has the slightest affection for even a venial sin.

To imagine that an indulgence must of necessity follow any prescribed act.

To fail to perform some of the works prescribed and yet imagine that one has gained the indulgence.

To remember that, properly, Communion should complete the works prescribed for an indulgence.

To imagine that sin is less heinous now than in former days, or that the Church so regards it, simply because the canonical penances have been abrogated.

To place any confidence in prayers found in Our Lord's sepulchre warranted to preserve from dying in an unnatural manner, and to be had from pious peddlers for ten cents. (There was no prayer found in Our Lord's sepulchre.)

To remember that one is guilty of a grievous sin of superstition who keeps any such prayer for the purposes intended, after correction.

All such foolish prayers should be destroyed.

16

The Correct Thing
When Calling on Clergymen

It is the Correct Thing

To remember that a clergyman's time is his gold-mine, and that no one has a right to trespass unduly long

To call during the hours set apart for visitors, so as to avoid taking him away from his work, study, or recreation.

To rise at the entrance of a clergyman, and to remain standing until he gives the signal to be seated.

If not invited to sit down, as may sometimes happen, to state one's business briefly, and withdraw.

If the call is merely a friendly one, to cut it short if there are others waiting to see the pastor.

If compelled to call at an unusual hour, meal-time, or late in the evening, to apologize for so doing and make the visit as brief as possible.

To avoid a loud tone when telling one's troubles to a priest, on the score both of breeding and prudence.

For members of a parish to make New Year's calls during the first weeks of the New Year on their pastor.

When calling on a bishop, to kneel down on one's left knee to kiss his ring and get his blessing.

To know that there is an indulgence attached to kissing a bishop's ring.

To leave one's card when calling on a clergyman who is not at home, when the call is a friendly one or on business

When the call is on business of purely a personal nature not to leave a card.

To remember that a clergyman has the right to give the signal for departure if he so desires, and that no offence should be taken if he does so.

It is Not the Correct Thing

To fail to remember one's pastor in his daily prayers.

To neglect to have the Holy Sacrifice of the Mass offered at times for the repose of the souls of deceased clergy: pastors, confessors, or directors. (How few show this mark of regard!)

To request a priest to offer Mass for a special intention or object without presenting an honorary. A priest is only bound to offer Mass for a special intention when this honorary is paid.

To forget that in the United States this honorary is never less than one dollar and may be any sum above this, according to one's regard for or obligations to the priest.

To ask a clergyman to perform any service incompatible with his sacred calling.

To borrow money from a clergyman, to ask him to endorse notes, or go security. A clergyman is not allowed to do these things.

To harass a clergyman for letters to officials, political or otherwise, to obtain employment.

To make long calls on busy clergymen.

To call late in the evening, at meal-times, before Mass, or right after dinner, on a clergyman.

To sit down in the presence of a clergyman without being asked to do so.

To selfishly keep others waiting whilst one enjoys a friendly chat.

To act as if one had a first mortgage on the time of a clergyman, and that no apology for an undue intrusion is ever necessary.

To make one's troubles audible to everyone who may chance to be in the house at the time one is seeking the advice of the pastor.

To ask the housekeeper questions about the regulations of the house and its expenditures.

To spend the time whilst waiting in looking at the books and papers which may be in the room.

To fail to send up one's name when calling on a clergyman.

To enter the parlor with muddy shoes, wet umbrella, or lighted cigar.

In Addressing Ecclesiastics

It is the Correct Thing

To give the proper title in speaking of Church dignitaries.

For Catholics living in the place where a bishop has jurisdiction to speak simply of "the bishop", "the archbishop", or "the cardinal".

For Catholics when visiting in the see of another bishop to speak of their own by name, as "Bishop Smith," or as "our bishop," or the "Bishop of Blankeville."

In Europe to be very punctilious in giving the correct titles.

To make use of the personal pronoun in the nominative case as seldom as possible in speaking of ecclesiastics. For example, "The archbishop was not feeling at all well last week; he intends to go to the seashore soon," would be more respectful, and therefore more correct, if changed to "The archbishop was not feeling at all well last week; His Grace intends to go to the seashore soon."

To know that a cardinal ranks with a prince.

An archbishop with a duke.

A bishop with an earl.

To know that this rank holds good even in Protestant countries, as is witnessed by the fact that the Prince of Wales has declared that Cardinal Manning should come next to himself on the Royal Commission.

In speaking of the pope to say "His Holiness," "The Holy Father," or in personal address, "Your Holiness."

Of a cardinal as "His Eminence," "Your Eminence."

Of an archbishop as "His Grace" or "Your Grace."

Of a bishop as "His Lordship" or "Your Lordship."

(These titles are not in common use in the United States.)

Address letters to an archbishop:

> Most Rev. (name in full), D.D.,
> Archbishop of (name of place)

To a bishop:

> Right Rev. (name), D.D.
> Bishop of (place)

To a rector :

> Rev. (name),
> Rector (name of church),
> Street

(A secular priest not a rector of a church is addressed as Rev. *Name*, with name of the church to which he is attached.)

To address members of religious communities in sacred orders as Rev. *Name*, then the initial letters designating the particular order.

The following are the titles and initials of religious orders approved in the United States:

Jesuit Fathers — S. J., meaning Society of Jesus.

Redemptorists Fathers — C.SS.R., Congregation of the Most Holy Redeemer.

Dominicans — O.P., Order of Preachers.

Franciscans — O.S.F., Order of St. Francis.

Benedictines — O.S.B., Order of St. Benedict.

Black Franciscans — O.M.C., Order of Minor Conventuals.

Augustinians — O.S.A., Order of St. Augustine.

Carmelites — O.C.C, Order of Caked Carmelites.

Servites — O.S., Order of Servites.

Capuchins — O.M. Cap., Order of Minor Capuchins.

Lazarists — CM., Congregation of the Mission.

Passionists — C.P., Congregation of the Passion.

Fathers of the Holy Cross — C.S.C., Congregation of the Holy Cross.

Paulists — C.S.P., Congregation of St. Paul.

Basilians — C.S.B., Congregation of St. Basil.

Resurrectionists — C.R., Congregation of the Resurrection.

Fathers of the Holy Ghost — C.S.Sp., Congregation of the Holy Ghost.

Fathers of the Precious Blood — C.PP.S., Congregation of the Most Precious Blood.

Fathers of St. Viatur — C.S.V., Congregation of St. Viatur.

Marists — S.M., Society of Mary.

Fathers of Mercy — S.P.M., Society of the Fathers of Mercy.

Oblates — O.M.I.,Oblates of Mary Immaculate.

Sulpitians — S.S., Saint Sulpice.

Religious communities of lay persons are addressed Brother or Sister. A Superior of a convent is usually called Mother, and the Superior General of an entire order of religious is called Reverend Mother.

It is Not the Correct Thing

To give a title to an ecclesiastic higher or lower than the one which is his due.

To say "Your Reverence" to a bishop, or "Your Eminence" to an archbishop.

To address a letter simply to "Bishop Smith," or "Father Smith."

To say "Father Bishop" or "Mr. Bishop," or "Father Priest" or "Mr. Priest."

To use a personal pronoun where the name or title could be substituted.

To reveal one's ignorance of their origin by criticizing the use of ecclesiastical titles.

When out of the diocese in which one lives, to speak of the bishop of one's place of residence as "the bishop," because one's auditors might naturally suppose that the bishop of their own city was meant.

18

The Correct Thing

For Members of Church Associations

It is the Correct Thing

For members of church associations to comply with the rules and regulations.

To be present if possible when meetings are called.

To have a certain amount of humility in regard to one's own ability.

To always withdraw at once from any organization which is not working in harmony with the pastor of the parish.

To refuse to accept an office if one is not willing and able to discharge its duties.

To remember that everybody cannot be first.

For sodalists to be punctual in saying their office.

To approach Holy Communion on the regular communion-days in a body.

For ladies to wear the veil, medal, and Sacred Heart badge where required to do so by the rules.

For gentlemen to comply with the regulations as regards uniforms.

To be prompt in paying all dues.

For members of a sewing-society to omit the usual quota of questionable gossip.

For the wealthy ladies of a parish to know that if they hold aloof from the benevolent organizations the great middle class will follow like a flock of geese, and that the burden of the expense and trouble will then fall on those who can least afford to bear it.

To know that there is really nothing contaminating in saying a few prayers and sewing in the same room with women who are "not in society."

To think more of the end to be attained than of the trouble in attaining it.

To be just before being generous.

It is Not the Correct Thing

To join an association and ignore its rules.

To be absent without sending a valid excuse to the secretary.

To belong to any society or organization which is not approved by the pastor.

To forget that wrangling and insubordination give scandal to the public, and that scandal is a sin for those who cause it.

To forget that there is work as well as honor attached to an office.

To withdraw because a perverse organization refuses to profit by one's superior wisdom.

For a sodalist to approach Holy Communion at an earlier or later Mass than the one named by the director of the sodality as the one at which the body of sodalists should approach the holy table.

To forget one's purse on Sundays when dues are in order.

To go to a sewing-society solely for the pleasure afforded.

For ladies of recognized position to refuse to lend their names to the furtherance of praiseworthy associations connected with their church.

To serve heaven with one's hands and the devil with one's tongue.

For ladies in charge of a fair to criticize the methods of their co-workers.

When soliciting for a fair or festival to be importunate in the matter of donations.

To promise a contribution and forget to send it afterwards.

For those called upon to act as if the solicitors were begging for themselves instead of the church.

To refuse a contribution in a discourteous manner.

To leave a solicitor standing in the hall whilst one makes up her mind whether she will give anything or not.

To give a donation as if conferring a personal favor on the one who solicits it.

To preface one's donation by the remarks that Father Blank is always begging; that Father Blank-Blank, the former pastor, thought of something besides money; that one would be glad to get into a parish where there were no debts, and where priests preached on the gospel instead of money, money all the time.

To head a subscription list with a large contribution to some charity enterprise when one's pew rent and church dues are unpaid.

The Correct Thing
In Business

It is the Correct Thing

To act as a gentleman in a business transaction, no matter how far his associate may forget himself.

To be scrupulously honest because it is right to be so, and not because "honesty is the best policy."

To remember that all rich men are not knaves nor all poor ones angels.

To make the best of one's opportunities.

To remember that a life need not necessarily be a failure because it is not crowned with wealth.

To be punctual to the second in keeping a business appointment.

To remember that a five minutes' delay has sometimes turned the tide of a young man's destiny.

To devote one's business hours strictly to business and one's time of recreation to something else.

To pay a good man what his services are worth, and not merely the minimum at which they can be obtained.

To avoid all misrepresentation in a business transaction.

To receive every one courteously, whether rich or poor, whom business brings to one's office.

To avoid all flippancy in a business transaction.

To remember that both master and men are subject to the same laws of right and wrong.

For business men to remember that a humane and considerate treatment of their employees ensures the respect of the general public as well as the approval of their own conscience.

To give a reproof, where necessary, in private.

For salesmen to remember that they are paid to wait upon customers, and are expected to act as gentlemen whether a purchase is made or not.

To remember that a frowning demeanor does not always imply a dignified one by any means.

For lawyers and doctors to remember that professional secrets are matters of honor, the betrayal of which, under any circumstance, would bring upon themselves the condemnation of the whole community.

For professional and business men to dress at all times as gentlemen.

For sorely-tried business men to remember that book-agents and peddlers are human, and sometimes reduced gentlefolk, and to therefore be as lenient as possible.

To hold one's word as sacred as one's bond.

To avoid all transactions that are classed in lump as shady.

To remember that adulation to power and arrogance to poverty mark a plebeian in mind as well as in origin.

To be manly at all times.

It is Not the Correct Thing

For a man to think that he can be a gentleman in the drawing-room and a boor in his office.

To consider ignorance in another as a warrant for one's own imposition upon him.

To question without good reason the business integrity of a man who grew suddenly rich, or to think that poverty is always a mark of uprightness and honesty and never of stupidity and want of business training.

To forget that in these days of gigantic investments, silver mines, railroads, western booms, and Yankee pluck, there is always an opportunity for the "hundredth man" to become rich.

To forget that fortune knocks once at every man's door, and sometimes only once.

To think that a fortune is necessary to happiness.

To forget that many of the world's greatest men died poor.

To forget that prudence as well as courtesy demands that one be punctual in keeping engagements.

To form irregular business habits.

To talk "shop" in society.

To devote one's whole life to business, to the neglect of spiritual and mental concerns.

To forget that employees when tempted into dishonesty sometimes salve their conscience with the thought of the bad example set by their employers.

To forget that money paid in salaries to deserving men is always a good investment.

To be a Shylock in demanding the whole of one's bond.

To think that misrepresentation in a business transaction is not a first cousin to stealing.

To have one code of manners for the rich and another for the poor.

To think that one's good manners which are only veneered will not break some day when, least expected or desired.

To act as if might made right.

For a man in society to imagine that the girl he may desire to marry is not perfectly familiar with his business reputation.

To think that a loud reproof in public is ever productive of any good.

To imagine that frigidity and intellect are synonymous terms.

To forget that quack doctors and pettifogging lawyers are known by a lack of honor, honesty, and integrity more than by a lack of ability.

For business and professional men to imitate gamblers, jockeys, and dudes in the matter of dress.

To think that antiquity in clothes adds dignity to one's profession.

To forget that agents sometimes carry articles that are worth purchasing.

To make use of technicalities to escape from one's just obligations.

To forget that one's shady transactions have an unfortunate habit of getting into the newspapers.

To imagine that a crime ever escapes unpunished.

To forget that ill-gotten gains will turn the downiest couch into a bed of thorns at the hour of death.

To forget that everybody admires a manly man.

20

The Correct Thing
For Business Women

It is the Correct Thing

To remember that work is not degradation.

That idleness under certain circumstances may be.

That a turn in the wheel of fortune is every day sending patricians to toil and plebeians to ease.

That the Blessed Virgin, the descendant of kings, the Mother of the King of kings, did not disdain either poverty or work.

That the world respects a woman who respects herself.

To be strictly on time in the school-room, office, or wherever one's duties call.

For a working-woman to remember that the time for which she is paid belongs to her employers.

To claim no indulgence on the score of gender.

To accept it gratefully if it is given.

To remember that employers as a rule prefer to discharge a woman rather than find fault with her.

To remember that prudence, patience, and perseverance are virtues particularly desirable in a business-woman.

To work only under reputable and honorable employers.

To insist at all times upon the respect due a lady.

To let one's conduct deserve it.

To be courteous and considerate of one's co-laborers.

To remember that courtesy to business associates does not imply a necessity of receiving them as friends if they are uncongenial, or one's social inferiors.

To be scrupulously neat and severely plain in attire.

To avoid jewelry, striking colors, pronounced styles, on the score of good taste as well as prudence.

To take proper care of one's physical health so as to avoid the "breakdown" which unfortunately usually overtakes the woman who is steadily employed.

To remember that one cannot work and be "in society" at the same time.

To find temporal happiness in home and friends, in books, music, art, flowers, and the pleasures which may be enjoyed in obscurity, and not sigh for social amusements beyond one's reach.

It is Not the Correct Thing

To prefer debt, difficulties, and starvation to work.

To imagine that all women of wealth and position have blue blood in their veins, and all women who work but the ordinary fluid.

For a woman to enter the bread-winning arena unless poverty compels her to do so.

To forget that some avocations are considered lady-like and others the reverse.

To get married solely to escape poverty and work.

To leave one's conscience at home when setting out for one's daily labors.

To imagine that God ever intended a woman to perform the same work as a man.

To dress in a manner incompatible with one's salary.

To be careless about one's personal appearance.

To imagine a costume cannot be tasteful and becoming without being very expensive.

To prefer two shabby gowns to one good one.

To say that one works for a living because one prefers to do so, and not because there is any want of the money earned, for everybody knows that such a statement is a rank falsehood.

To imagine that it would be to one's credit if it were true, since some other woman who needs the money would be kept out of the position.

For women who merely wish to make some pin-money to work for less than the regular rates, since by so doing they reduce the wages of those who must earn their daily bread.

For women in comfortable circumstances to imagine that there is nothing dishonest and dishonorable in sending embroidery, paintings, and fancy articles to be disposed of at the Exchanges intended only to help those really in need of such assistance.

For women in general to forget that man's inhumanity to man is sometimes but a shadow compared to woman's inhumanity to woman.

21

The Correct Thing
For Office Hours

It is the Correct Thing

To remember that man was made for the office, not the office for man.

To do nothing as a politician that one would scorn to do in private life.

To know that the man who makes his office the stepping-stone to wealth and advancement for all his relatives and friends, deserves, and generally gets, the opprobrium of all honorable people.

To remember that the maxim "A public office is a public trust" is not altogether obsolete except among professional politicians.

To pledge nothing as a candidate which one is not prepared to fulfill when in office.

To remember that the sins of all the generations since Adam are visited by the opposition press on the heads of candidates for office.

To be as affable and as concerned about the life, liberty, and pursuit of happiness of one's constituents after election as one was before.

To remember that there is no office in the world worth the sacrifice of honor and honesty.

For an office-holder to be as anxious about his public work as he was about his private concerns.

To remember that his duty is to the public at large, who pay the taxes, and not to the party that elected him.

To devote his time to the discharge of official duties, and not in ladling out spoils to political henchmen.

It is Not the Correct Thing

To imagine that offices were created by benevolent statesmen to give employment to professional politicians.

To forget that popular elections sometimes lack a good deal of being popular.

To imagine that in electing one man to office the people intended to also elect all his "brothers and his cousins and his uncles," etc.

To imagine that a man is not answerable as a man for sins committed as an office-holder.

To enter politics if one's past history will not bear a calcium light.

To win votes under false pretenses and through misrepresentations.

To imagine that "mud-throwing" is a dignified or gentlemanly way of conducting a campaign.

To use one's office for gain other than in a legitimate way.

To talk about the "brotherhood of man" at mass meetings and ignore the needs of the people when in office.

To prefer re-election to office to the welfare of the people at large and the approval of one's own conscience.

The Correct Thing
For a Citizen

It is the Correct Thing

For a citizen to remember that he owes a duty to the community in which he lives.

To know the difference between statesmanship and political wire-pulling.

To remember that a trickster holding office is a standing reproach to the community which permitted his election.

To know that a bad law does not bind in conscience.

Before saying too much about the State to have a fair idea of the men who happen, for all practical purposes, to be "the State."

To remember that parents and citizens as individuals have certain functions as individuals which cannot be thrown off upon the State.

To let love of country be second only to love of God.

To know that the very least a loyal son of his country can do is to cast his vote for good men, and to help elect statesmen and gentlemen, and not ward politicians and tricksters.

To remember that a reputable citizen who accepts office deserves the gratitude of every other reputable citizen.

To take a patriotic pride in the prosperity of one's country, one's State, and one's city.

To contribute cheerfully to all public enterprises.

To remember that a bad Christian never made a good citizen.

To answer in the negative Scott's immortal question:

"Breathes there a man with soul so dead
Who never to himself has said
This is my own, my native land?"

For a man to think that he can rightfully live only for himself.

To claim the benefits of citizenship, and to shirk its burdens.

To think that rights have not their corresponding obligations.

To imagine that it is unworthy of a gentleman to take an interest in politics.

To think that a man entitled to the ballot, who holds aloof from the polls and then talks about political corruption, is not partly to blame for such a state of affairs.

To forget that in some instances "the State" which a few would have us believe is infallible, is composed, as far as real power is concerned, of many political tricksters who use public trusts and public funds to further personal and party ends.

To forget that good men sometimes break bad laws.

To talk about political corruption when one does nothing to mend the matter.

To forget that the "State" was made for man, not man for the State.

To imagine that admiration and approval are acceptable substitutes for money in public and charitable enterprises.

23

The Correct Thing
In Society

It is the Correct Thing

To discharge one's social obligations faithfully.

To pay especial deference to elderly people wherever met.

To be punctilious in calling upon and sending invitations to one's friends who have become reduced in circumstances, otherwise one lays herself liable to the suspicion that she values her friends for their wealth and social position.

To seek the society of those only who are congenial, since one has a right to choose one's friends.

To be pleasant to everyone whom one accidentally meets.

To remember that ladies of assured position can afford to be democratic, in the selection of their guests if they so desire, and that it is only the parvenues who are constantly revising their calling lists.

For those in society to observe social usages.

To remember that there are a great many people who, like the old Israelites, worship the golden calf.

To make a point of saying a few pleasant words to those who seem to be neglected at a large reception.

For kind-hearted Catholic matrons to chaperon motherless girls to places of amusement.

To remember that people of the highest rank are generally the least haughty.

For every well-born, well-bred American to act as if she felt herself the equal of every other well-bred, well-born American, regardless of fortune.

To remember that snobs and parvenues would not receive St. Peter himself unless he came with the proper credentials.

To get rid of undesirable acquaintances in some other manner besides the "cut direct."

To have many acquaintances, but few friends.

To refuse to introduce people who belong to different social grades.

To consider a friend's roof as sufficient introduction at the time.

To assist cheerfully in affairs gotten up for charity through motives of charity, and not merely because it is fashionable to do so.

For ladies in society to use their position to further charitable aims.

For the rich to remember that money from them would be more acceptable than encouraging words.

For the poor to be generous with their sympathy and praise.

To remember that men may have been born equal at the time of the Declaration of Independence, but that they did not remain so. That women never were.

To understand that in the absence of a written peerage, social position in America is a good deal a matter of geography. That in some places birth, breeding, and beauty are the determining factors; in most places it is money, and in some instances it is mere luck, and that therefore a high place is too uncertain to run any spiritual risks to obtain.

To refuse to know people who have forfeited their right in respectable society, whatever may be their position.

To think twice twenty times before uttering a word that would tarnish a girl's reputation.

To remember that legacy hunters are sometimes disappointed.

That rich relations have, as a rule, an average amount of sense, and are generally good readers of character.

To have a convenient memory at times.

To remember that money given in charity is on interest in heaven.

To entertain in accordance with one's means.

For a matron to refuse to present a man whom she would not care to have meet her own daughters, to the daughters of other people.

To be conspicuous by one's absence from indelicate or suggestive plays.

To be blind at times in art galleries.

To refuse to discuss certain books, certain plays, and certain pictures with gentlemen.

For both maids and matrons to understand that some décolleté gowns are correct, some are immodest, and some are indecent.

To remember that lace, gauze, and tulle are unfailing friends to both the stout woman and to the thin one: to the first on the score of modesty, to the second on that of beauty.

For a thin woman to understand that angles unadorned are not adorned the most.

For a Catholic to refuse to dance round dances if she has conscientious scruples in the matter.

To understand that some dances were never intended to be danced in refined circles.

To refuse to dance with a man whose reputation is not above reproach, no matter under whose roof he happens to be.

For a gentleman to be moderate in his use of wine at a party or reception.

To remember that a man who feels in the slightest degree "his cups" has no place in a social gathering and should take his departure on short order.

For a Catholic to refuse chicken salad and other meats at a party supper after twelve o'clock on Thursday night.

To say the principal part of one's regular prayers before going to an evening entertainment.

To carefully refrain from doing or saying anything that would wound the feelings or reputation of another.

To let one's good manners be the natural outcome of a good heart, and not merely a veneering of social form.

For an uninteresting girl to remember that men are not usually actuated by motives of philanthropy in going to a party, and that if she objects to being merely a looker-on in Vienna she must make herself attractive.

For good-hearted gentlemen to pay some attention to "wall-flowers", both as a courtesy to their hostess and as a kindness to their sisters in Mother Eve.

For the rich to spend their money to give pleasure to their friends.

For a Catholic girl to be a model in society to all others.

It is Not the Correct Thing

To give up the greater part of one's time to social duties.

To reserve one's most winning manners for the rich and those in high places.

To forget in prosperity the friends in adversity.

To forget that old friends, like old wines, are generally the best.

To toady to wealth, to be supercilious to poverty.

To be too familiar with equals.

To forget that an angel was once entertained unawares.

To be eccentric in regard to conforming to social usages

To be ashamed of one's religion.

To introduce religious discussions in society.

To be a self-constituted Little Sister of the Rich.

To ignore the presence of a stranger or a "wall flower" at a reception.

In making up an opera party to include only the reigning belles.

For a girl to introduce the stupid men to her friends and to keep the agreeable ones for herself.

To remember the faults and forget the virtues of one's friends.

To forget to be careful in forming acquaintances, more careful in selecting friends, and most careful in choosing confidants.

For a girl to have secrets she would not care to tell her mother or guardian.

For a girl's conduct, however harmless, to be such as would call out unpleasant comment.

To patronize only charitable affairs that are fashionable and leave the others to take care of themselves.

To make a charity entertainment the occasion of "envy, malice, and all uncharitableness".

To think more of one's own part than of the object to be attained.

For a girl to take all the pleasure and credit in a charitable entertainment, and shirk all the work.

For a woman to try to make a charity organization the stepping-stone to social advancement.

To speak on all occasions possible of "my third cousin, Mr. Croesus," and to ignore the existence of "my uncle, Mr. Poorman."

For a woman in moderate circumstances to try to entertain on the same scale as her wealthy friends.

For people to live beyond their means.

For a young man working on a salary to emulate the example of his wealthier associates.

For a woman to cheat the grocer in order to dress her daughters in silk attire and a sealskin jacket.

For a young man to spend half his salary for flowers and opera tickets for a rich girl, who may accept the attentions gracefully, but will be very far from accepting the man who offers them.

For a girl to accept valuable presents from gentlemen.

For a consistent Catholic to permit any attentions whatever from a divorced man, and only what is conscientiously proper from any married man.

To devote more time to social pleasures than to religious and home duties.

To think that a few prayers hurried through at three o'clock in the morning, when one is half asleep, constitute a proper night prayer.

For a girl to be on the constant look-out for a rich husband. She is generally disappointed.

For a woman to ignore the opinion of her husband, father, or brother, in regard to the proper cut of an evening bodice.

To wear an immodest gown because somebody else happens to.

To call a girl who refuses to dance round dances a prude.

To dance so much as to injure one's health.

For those who practice the old-fashioned custom of keeping open house on New Year's day to offer wine to their callers.

TO FORGET THAT TIME IS BUT A PRELUDE TO ETERNITY.

The Correct Thing
In Conversation

It is the Correct Thing

To remember that, according to the old philosophers, speech is silver, and silence is golden.

To remember that those who think twice before they speak, and in some instances do not speak at all, save themselves many after regrets.

To remember that mere talk lacks a great deal of being conversation.

To remember that personalities are ill-bred.

To listen respectfully to old people and those whose position entitles them to consideration.

To avoid talking scandal and gossip.

To avoid coarseness in conversation as one would the leprosy.

To remember that stabbing one's body is not half so great a crime as stabbing one's reputation.

To remember the Golden Rule and do unto others as you would have them do unto you, when tempted to repeat an ill-natured or compromising bit of gossip.

To remember that women, old and young, married and single, who indulge in indelicate and coarse expressions, double entendres, and select topics for conversation which they would blush to have overheard by gentlemen, have forfeited all right to the title of ladies, to say nothing of that of Christians.

To manifest marked displeasure when indelicate and immodest subjects are broached.

To frown down all mention even of salacious books and newspaper scandals. Good breeding as well as delicacy requires this.

To speak deferentially to superiors, kindly to inferiors, and courteously to equals.

To remember that if you cannot keep your own secrets, it is hardly fair to expect your friends to keep them for you.

To remember that slander is a grievous sin.

To remember that religious discussions in general conversation are usually productive of but little good.

To explain patiently, clearly, and lucidly any point connected with the Church to those who are sincere in seeking information.

If unable to give a clear answer, to say so at once, and not run the risk of giving a false impression in what might prove a serious matter.

Decline all arguments with a professional infidel.

> "A man convinced against his will
> Remains of the same opinion still."

To correct patiently and courteously any misstatement made in regard to the Church or her history.

For a person who mingles much in cultivated society to be familiar with the Catholic position in regard to the leading questions of the day, and to be "loaded and primed" conversationally when the occasion demands.

To remain always calm, cool, and collected in an argument.

For a Catholic to offer to loan suitable books to one seeking information, and then decline, if he feels like it, any further discussion at the time.

To practice Hannibal's tactics and carry the war into Africa, in an argument; in other words, to ask an explanation of the creed of an opponent rather than spend all one's force in defending one's own.

To remember that a fool can ask more questions in a minute than a wise man can answer in an hour.

It is Not the Correct Thing

To keep one's tongue in constant use.

To talk whether one understands the subject of conversation or not.

To forget that a good listener is appreciated quite as much as a good conversationalist.

To be an animated newspaper.

To talk of private affairs in public places.

To laugh at coarse jests, and to take part or to listen to indelicate conversations.

To repeat scandal.

To make thoughtless remarks as to the age, past history, social position, family skeletons, financial embarrassments, absurdity in dress, peculiarity in speech or behavior, or anything which would wound the feelings of another.

To argue in society.

To meekly acquiesce, for fear of giving offense, to a slander or misstatement in regard to the Church.

To speak in a loud tone.

To get unduly excited over an argument.

To discuss religious questions flippantly.

To attempt to explain to an opponent what one does not thoroughly understand one's self.

To "pump" children and servants in order to find out the private affairs of one's neighbors.

To forget that a piece of scandal put in circulation at a sewing society or an afternoon tea is harder to recall than a bag of feathers scattered to the four winds in a Kansas cyclone.

To damn a rival with faint praise.

To use slang.

To speak disrespectfully of the religious convictions of any one in his presence.

To criticize clergymen and religious. In the first place, there is danger of giving scandal; and in the second, it is a want of Christian charity to hold up the faults of those who have sacrificed their lives for the salvation of souls

To forget that it is only vulgar, ill-bred people who talk scandal, gossip, unkind personalities, on indelicate topics, slang, in a loud voice, are careless of the feelings of others, and bore people with arguments and bluster.

To forget that cultivated and Christian people are affable, amiable, elegant, refined, delicate, considerate, and pleasing in conversation.

To forget that books, music, art, social happenings, political complications, ethical questions, scientific researches, fashions, household decoration, travel, projects and plans, sanitary improvements, charitable institutions, literary and social clubs, fads, fancies, and foibles afford plenty of material for harmless and instructive conversation.

To forget that an account will have to be one day rendered of every idle word.

The Correct Thing
In Matters of Dress

It is the Correct Thing

To dress according to one's means.

To avoid all extremes and eccentricities in dress.

To remember that neatness, scrupulous cleanliness, and a perfect fit are the fundamentals in a proper attire.

To pay dressmakers and seamstresses a fair price for their work.

To pay them promptly.

To avoid conspicuous attire on the street.

To dress in society as the occasion demands.

For rich people to wear costly apparel.

For poor ones and those in moderate circumstances to avoid

unpleasant comment by wearing inexpensive gowns in which good taste and a graceful style compensate for the want of cost.

To remember that one of the marks of a lady is to dress as one.

To keep one's clothes in perfect order.

To make a liberal use of soap and water.

To remember that male cranks wear their hair long and female cranks theirs short.

To leave rouge to the green-room where it is a necessary adjunct, and to the women who have no reputation to be compromised.

To remember that tight lacing, and any device of the toilet which injures the health, is not only bad taste, but is a positive sin.

To remember that no lady, to say nothing of a Catholic worthy of the name, will wear a gown cut immodestly low.

To dress becomingly in the home circle.

To remember that the body is the temple of the Holy Ghost, and is therefore worthy of proper care.

26

The Correct Thing

TO THINK LESS OF ADORNING THE BODY THAN THE SOUL.

It is Not the Correct Thing

For a woman to spend more than she can afford on dress.

For a woman to spend the greater part of her time shopping, studying fashion-plates, devising costumes, and sewing.

For a woman who can afford better to wear shabby gowns.

To follow an ugly and unbecoming fashion.

For poor women to try to rival rich ones in matters of dress.

To haggle over a reasonable price for dress-making and sewing.

To show disrespect to a hostess by appearing at her entertainments in unsuitable apparel.

To wear showy and expensive costumes at church.

To wear shabby costumes at church, as if anything were good enough for the house of God.

To wear torn stockings, ripped gloves, shoes with buttons off, gowns in need of dusting and renovating, hats out of date and unbecoming, soiled collars, cuffs, or ruching, and to make a liberal use of pins.

To use rouge on the cheeks, ink on the eye-brows, or blondine on the hair.

To use powder too freely. Its proper use is merely to take the shiny appearance off the face after it has been washed, or when going out in the wind and sun to prevent chapping.

To forget that an immodest gown is a mark of low breeding.

To devote the greater part of one's time to the consideration of clothes.

To think that anything is good enough to wear at home.

For a woman to appear in the home circle in a slouchy wrapper, old slippers, hair disheveled, bangs in curl-papers, or in a worn-out reception gown sadly in need of repairs.

To forget that art in many instances may remedy the defects of nature.

To let vanity be the motive in taking proper care of the body.

27

The Correct Thing
In the Street

It is the Correct Thing

To appear dressed neatly, soberly, and becomingly on the street.

To avoid every act calculated to attract attention.

To return all salutations courteously.

To avoid what is called a street flirtation as one would the plague.

To remember that laughter and loud tones are particularly unbecoming on the street.

To remember that others have the right of way as well as one's self, and that it is ill-bred to try to monopolize the whole pavement.

To refrain from staring at the passers-by.

To remember that no lady is ever seen talking on the street-corner.

To remember that the street is not a dining-room for the consumption of candy, peanuts, etc.

For a younger person to give precedence to an older one.

It is Not the Correct Thing

To wear flashy, showy costumes, jewelry, or rouge on the street. To be dressed so shabbily as to attract attention.

To be defective in eyesight when a poor acquaintance is passing by.

For a girl to try to attract a gentleman's attention.

To speak to someone across the street.

To hold an umbrella so that its drippings will fall upon one's companion or the passing pedestrians.

For three or four girls to walk abreast like a detachment of militia, to the inconvenience of others who have a right to the street.

For a lady to take a gentleman's arm in the day-time unless it has been sleeting.

For a girl to giggle, talk slang, or discuss private affairs on the street.

To laugh at the defects or the peculiarities of persons seen on the street.

To show ill-temper if one is jostled by the crowd.

28

The Correct Thing
In the Street Cars

It is the Correct Thing

For a lady to thank a gentleman who relinquishes his seat for her in a low, well-bred, courteous tone of voice.

To occupy no more space than is necessary in a crowded car.

For a lady courteously to refuse a seat offered by an elderly gentleman or a tired working man.

For a lady to offer her seat to an elderly person, an invalid, or a woman with a baby.

To have the fare ready so as not to keep the conductor waiting.

To avoid audible comments on one's fellow-passengers.

For those nearest the box to offer to deposit the fare on cars where the company is too poor to provide conductors.

To be ready with a gracious apology if one is compelled to stumble over others in reaching a seat.

It is Not the Correct Thing

For a lady to flounce into a vacated seat as if it were her right, with an inaudible "thank you", or none at all, to the gentleman who voluntarily relinquished it for her.

For a lady to take possession of a seat vacated for another one.

For a young lady of leisure to remain selfishly seated when weary working-people are standing, exhausted by their day's labor.

To fumble through pocket and purse for the desired fare instead of having it conveniently ready.

To crowd and push against others.

To "look daggers" at one who unavoidably steps on one's toes or gown.

To read letters in a street-car, unless it is desired to have others acquainted with their contents.

To ridicule fellow-passengers.

To mention names in a conversation on the cars.

In Shopping

It is the Correct Thing

For a person to spend a reasonable length of time looking at the articles displayed in the stores without purchasing anything, if she finds nothing to suit her fancy or her purse.

To ask politely to be shown what one is in search of, as it is the business of the employees to wait upon customers.

To take as much time as is necessary in making a purchase.

To remember that it is the salesmen's business to sell goods, and that they are therefore not likely to be disinterested advisers.

To comply with the regulations of the shop in regard to the exchanging of goods.

To avoid a supercilious air in dealing with the salespeople.

To avoid familiarities in manner or speech in dealing with them.

To say "thank you" at the conclusion of a transaction.

To thank courteously the salesman who has been waiting on one where no purchase has been made.

To avoid making the aisles of the big stores the rendezvous for meeting all one's acquaintances.

It is Not the Correct Thing

To make a tour of the shops, pulling down and examining goods, pricing articles, and taking up the time of the salesmen, when there is no intention of purchasing anything.

To haggle over the price of articles.

To tell the salesman that the same thing can be purchased cheaper at another store. If that is the case, quietly say that the article is not what is wanted (as it is not, at that price), and then go to the more reasonable shop and make the desired purchase.

To so far forget the demeanor of a lady as to indulge in contradictions as to the merits of goods with the salesman.

To forget that courtesy is due to a working-woman as much as to any one else.

To make a practice of dropping into stores where tea and other refreshments are being served. These are intended for the customers and not for the general public.

To ask a lady returned from a shopping expedition the prices of the various articles purchased. She may have objections to telling their cost.

To tell falsehoods about the cost of an article.

The Correct Thing
When Traveling

It is the Correct Thing

To remember that one of the surest tests of a lady is her ability to travel as one.

To be properly attired when traveling.

To avoid wearing garments that are conspicuous in any way.

To remember that fellow-passengers have rights as well as one's self.

To open or close a window if the doing so would add to the comfort of others.

For a lady to travel alone in America if necessity demands it.

For a young lady to refuse decidedly and at once to enter into any sort of conversation with obtrusive strangers.

For a lady to answer courteously any questions which may be put to her by an elderly person.

To assist in any way in her power a country-woman, or one unused to traveling.

To provide one's self with time-tables, maps, etc., so as to be independent in the matter of information in regard to the route.

To make the best of the situation if compelled to share one's seat.

To remember that the porter in a sleeping-car can only make up one berth at a time, regardless of his good intentions or tips.

To explain lucidly and decidedly, but without any show of temper or ill-breeding, a mistake or imposition of which one has been the victim.

For a girl to remember that giggling, loud laughter, shrill tones, personalities, family history made public, *tête-à-têtes* with strange young men, excite the disgust of everybody on the train with her as well as of the very ones who help her to make a fool of herself.

To remember that one is not excused from night and morning prayers simply because one happens to be on a journey.

To remember that other travelers have as much right to the dressing-room as one's self, and therefore it should not be occupied for an indefinite length of time.

To take one's good manners and Christian principles along with one, instead of packing them away with one's wardrobe.

It is Not the Correct Thing

To think that one can have one code of manners when traveling and another for home use.

For a lady to wear silk gowns, gay colors, flaring hats, or other conspicuous apparel when traveling.

To remember that a true lady is happiest when attracting the least attention.

To selfishly open a window when a person with asthma or consumption is sitting opposite.

For a lady to make a practice of going on long journeys alone.

For a young lady who respects herself to permit any advances from strange young men.

To answer snappishly, or not all, questions politely put to one.

To be constantly troubling the conductor with questions as to the route, etc.

To make fellow-passengers nervous by talking audibly about wrecks, explosions, etc.

To think that one can do with impunity when abroad what one would not do at home.

To look daggers at a person compelled to share one's seat. The stranger probably regrets the intrusion quite as much as one's self.

To think that one is entitled to a whole section who has only paid for one berth.

To make a circus of one's self and one's temper, for the benefit of disgusted or amused fellow-travelers, over mistakes and misunderstandings.

To forget that others besides poor Goldsmith think that "the loud laugh bespeaks a vacant mind".

For a girl tempted into conversations with strange men to forget Weller's advice on matrimony: "Don't."

To think that the law of abstinence from meat on Friday is abrogated simply because one happens to be traveling.

To scatter the debris of one's lunch around the seat to the annoyance and disgust of others.

To lock one's self in the dressing-room and proceed to make one's toilet as leisurely as if at home, regardless of others, who have some excuse for wishing their selfish companion in Timbuktu or the tropics.

To wear one's shabbiest manners along with one's shabbiest gown when traveling.

31

The Correct Thing
In the Home Circle

It is the Correct Thing

To remember that every one who has a happy home, be it humble or grand, is rich.

To be courteous, considerate, affable, and entertaining at home as well as in society.

For a man to be as attentive to his wife as he was to his fiancée

For a woman to be as fascinating after marriage as she was before.

For a man to consider that money spent to give pleasure to his wife and family is money well spent.

For a woman to understand that on her shoulders usually rests the burden of domestic economy, and to shape her expenditures in accordance with her income.

For a man to really be a woman's intellectual superior if he wants to be considered so.

For a wife to understand that a woman in a shabby gown, with untidy hair, dull eyes, uncared-for complexion, and a peevish manner, is not usually regarded as the most pleasing ornament at the head of a man's table.

For a man to bear in mind that no woman is going to love a man very deeply whom she cannot respect.

For a woman to remember that a smile of welcome, a becoming toilet, an inviting home, a well-cooked and daintily-served dinner, are no more than what is due to a man who has worked hard all day for her and their children.

For a man to speak of having won his wife's affections and not of her as having won his, no matter what may be the facts in the case.

For a woman to remember that it is those calm, even-tempered, prosaic, common-sense sort of women who are the real masters in the home, no matter who enjoys the nominal honor, and that those who are "bundles of nerves and electricity" only wear themselves out with their storms and tears without gaining anything, unless it be a bit of lofty advice.

For both husband and wife to remember that the marriage vows are solemn things which should be solemnly kept.

For both to "bear and forbear" with each other.

To remember that a home without God cannot long be a happy one.

For a man who remains out at his "club" until after twelve o'clock at night to expect to find his wife in temper and tears when he finally reaches home.

For attractive young wives to remember that a "married flirt" always brings upon herself the condemnation of society if the condemnation of her own conscience does not keep her within the bounds of propriety.

For a woman to make home pleasant.

For a man to show his appreciation of her efforts.

For every member of a household to remember that punctuality is a virtue to be practiced daily, and in small matters as well as in the more important ones.

For every room in the house to be as attractive in its way as the parlor.

To know that open-handed hospitality is generally rewarded by the happiness afforded, even in this world.

To know that great men and noble women are generally reared in happy homes.

To remember that courtesy, patience, consideration, affability, self-sacrifice, sympathy, are some of the virtues to be practiced in the home circle.

To have family prayers in common where possible.

For every member of a household to consider morning prayer as much of a duty as prayers at night.

To be punctilious about saying grace before meals, and returning thanks afterwards.

To let no unpleasant subject ever be broached at table.

To be ever ready and glad to give a place at one's board to a friend.

To be temperate in eating as well as in drinking.

For a Christian "To eat to live, not live to eat."

For a Catholic to serve Friday fare on Friday, no matter who is expected to dine.

To have a crucifix in every bedroom.

To have Catholic engravings or paintings in the parlors as well as in bedrooms.

For children to love, honor, and obey their parents.

For parents to teach children their prayers as soon as they are able to talk.

To be careful that children never see nor hear anything that could tarnish their innocence in the slightest degree.

To take care that children are not frightened by stones of ghosts and hobgoblins.

To punish them when they need correction.

To be kind but firm always with children.

To watch over their associations.

To answer their questions accurately.

To understand their faults as well as their perfections.

To let them dress as children, partake of the amusements of children, be obedient as children, think as children, learn as children, be innocent as children.

To remember that a "grown-up child" is a disgusting as well as a sorrowful spectacle.

To understand that precocity is not talent.

To remember the old maxim about the twig and the tree.[12]

To celebrate both the birthdays and the feasts of the patron saints of the several members of the family, as well as all other family feasts, since it tends to foster a love of family and of home.

It is Not the Correct Thing

To think that only the rich can have happy homes.

To lay aside good manners with one's best clothes, to be used only in society.

For a chivalrous admirer to develop into a boorish and indifferent husband.

For a beautiful, fascinating girl to unmask as a commonplace, ugly wife.

To imagine that little quarrels never develop into big ones.

For a man to dole out his money to his wife as if it were wartime rations.

For a man who spends money for cigars, wines, expensive luncheons, club-dues, newspapers, suppers, and baseball, to find fault if his wife indulges in candy, concerts, flowers, magazines, pretty clothes, and insists on entertaining her friends.

For a woman to plan her housekeeping on a scale beyond her income.

---

12   "As the twig is bent, so is the tree inclined." Proverbial saying, early 18th century; meaning that early influences have a permanent effect. There is a related comment of the mid 16th century, 'a man may bend a wand while it is green and make it straight though it be never so crooked,' but the current form comes originally from Alexander Pope's Epistles to Several Persons (1732): "'Tis education forms the common mind, Just as the twig is bent the tree's inclined.'

To sacrifice comfort for the sake of keeping up appearances.

For a woman to imagine that her neighbors care particularly whether she keeps one servant or a dozen.

To forget that it is an utter impossibility to please everybody, and that if one pleases one's self and one's household there is a certainty of pleasing somebody.

For a man to imagine that he knows more than his wife, simply because he happens to be a man.

For a woman to neglect her personal appearance at home, reserving all her taste and trouble for society.

To imagine that children raised in an atmosphere of wrangling, temper, selfishness, and coldness are not going to develop traits in keeping with their surroundings.

To be discourteous, overbearing, selfish, blunt, and cold in the home circle.

To think family prayers are obsolete.

To act as if the day belonged to one's self and need not be sanctified by prayer, and that only at night is the assistance of God required.

To think that grace before meals should only be said in convents, and that worldlings, like horses, are excused.

To make the dinner-table the tribunal for hearing all the family complaints.

To consider hospitality among the obsolete virtues.

To be a gourmand at table.

To act as if one took an especial delight in eating.

To serve meat on Friday at a Catholic table (hotels excepted).

For children to rule their parents and the household.

For children to be able to speak "pieces" before they are able to say their prayers.

To permit a profane word or a doubtful conversation before children.

To allow children to have the immodest or coarse pictures which unfortunately are only too plentiful.

To have vulgar paintings in the parlors.

To allow nurses to frighten children in their charge in any way.

To forget that many a child has been made nervous for life because of early frights.

To punish a child because one is angry, and not because it needs correction.

To imagine that one's own children for some occult reason are created brighter, better, and smarter than the children of any one else.

To think that children who are not taught to be truthful, upright, honorable, and courteous will grow so naturally.

To think that children will outgrow their faults, and to forget that they may outgrow their virtues.

To be spasmodic and changeable in dealing with children.

To forget that children acquire their earliest information through persistent questioning.

To forget that bad associations corrupt good manners.

To imagine that it is not a very serious thing to be responsible for the spiritual as well as the temporal welfare of a child.

To permit children to think more of dress than of their games, to ape the manners of young ladies and gentlemen.

To talk about their engagements, their admirers, their conquests; to permit them to think disobedience a small matter; to have them interested in subjects which belong to an adult period; to let anything ever come into their lives which would tarnish the bloom of childish innocence.

To mistake for "smartness" what others may call impertinence.

To forget the old saying, that a mother's rarest jewels are her children.

To neglect to send children to church and school as soon as they are able to go.

To send children to any other than a Catholic school.

32

The Correct Thing
In Dealing with Servants

It is the Correct Thing

To remember that servants are human beings with human feelings and human weaknesses.

To insist that servants should do their work thoroughly and punctually.

To be kind and considerate to them, and to teach children to be the same.

To remember that a word of kindly interest in their affairs costs little, and may be productive of much benefit.

To be ever ready to praise where praise is deserved.

To administer reproof and correction, where necessary, in private, and in a calm, firm manner.

To remember that it is lowering to one's dignity to give way to anger to a servant, no matter how much provoked.

To discharge a servant peremptorily for grave impertinence or direct disobedience.

To see that each servant under one's charge goes to Mass on Sundays and holy days, to confession at regular times, and to encourage them to belong to sodalities.

To know that this is not a mere counsel, but a solemn duty, and that a master or mistress who neglects it commits sin.

To encourage them to read good books.

To see that they have a comfortable room.

To look after their welfare should they get sick in one's service.

To encourage them to save their wages instead of spending money foolishly, or making uncertain investments.

To permit them certain times for recreation.

To know what company they keep.

To see that they have enough to eat.

To forbid waste.

To be patient in training them into one's particular ways.

To remember that a girl coming from a peasant's abode in Europe cannot be expected to know even the names, to say nothing of the use, of certain articles in a refined household.

To remember that it is dishonorable to entice a good servant away from an acquaintance by the promise of higher wages or easier hours; and that in many instances the neighbor in question would mind it less if one walked off with a piece of bric-a-brac from her parlor table, for money could replace the one, whilst for the other there might be plenty of trouble in getting a substitute.

To imitate the example of the chatelaines of old in their management of servants.

It is Not the Correct Thing

To forget that good servants are not born, but are generally made through much patience and hard work.

To allow servants to be lax, tardy, and slothful in doing their work.

To be capricious, whimsical, and tyrannical with servants, or to allow children to be so.

To forget that in this day and time a good servant is a treasure, and that an overbearing mistress may count on "receiving warning".

To treat servants as if they were mere automatons to one's bidding.

To scold servants before other people.

To reprove for a trifle when one is vexed, and let what is grievous pass unnoticed when one is in good humor.

To forget one's dignity on any occasion with servants.

To be totally oblivious of their aches and pains and troubles.

To accept exemplary service as one's due without a word of kindly appreciation, even if one does pay for the service.

To forget that many pay good wages and but few get good service.

To forget that impertinence unpunished demoralizes one's authority.

To be careless and neglectful about seeing to the religious duties of one's servants.

To arrange one's household and meal-hours on Sunday so as to make it extremely difficult, if not impossible, for servants to get to Mass.

To forget that a servant who is not faithful to God is not going to be faithful to an employer.

To permit them to have, or to read immoral and worthless books and papers in one's house.

To allow them to remain out late at night.

To put servants in damp, dark, illy-ventilated, cold rooms.

To turn a servant out on the world who gets sick in one's service.

To allow them to keep questionable company whilst in one's service.

To imagine that servants who work hard and have tolerably healthy constitutions can live on air and a few leavings from the household table.

To think that it is not a mild sort of stealing to entice a good servant away from someone else.

The Correct Thing

In Education

It is the Correct Thing

To remember that a true education must be physical, mental, and spiritual.

For parents to educate their children.

To know that mere instruction may lack a great deal of being education.

To know that animals can be instructed, but that only human beings can be educated.

To know that if a child cannot learn mathematics by intuition, it cannot learn religion in that way either.

To know that education is the training, developing, and perfecting of one's powers.

To remember that a little learning is a dangerous thing.

To favor that system of education which makes good Christians, good citizens, and good members of a family.

For the State to compel parents to give their children an education which will train them to be competent voters, loyal citizens, and useful members of a community.

To know that children belong to their parents and not to the State.

For parents to know that they are bound in conscience to give their children an education suitable to their station in life.

To know that an education which ignores the soul is defective and un-Christian.

To know that a large percentage of the criminals in the United States were trained in non-religious schools.

For every child of Christian parents to be given a Christian education as its right.

To know that a whole community cannot justly be made to pay for that which only a part can in conscience use.

For the State to assume the duties of educator only where the parents or guardians fail to do their duty.

It is Not the Correct Thing

To educate a child as if its existence were to end with the grave.

For parents to shirk their responsibilities towards their children on the public.

To imagine that a child which has been instructed in certain arts and sciences and sent to a gymnasium is educated.

To expect a descendant of Adam to be good, and loyal, and conscientious, and firm in the hour of trial, and strict in the performance of every duty simply because it is natural to be so. Too confiding victims may learn better by sad experience.

For the average college graduate to think that there is nothing more for him to learn.

To forget that the usual way of judging a tree is by its fruits.

For the extremely fallible men who compose the State to interfere in the education of children whose parents or guardians are doing all that is necessary in that regard.

To forget that people must exist before the State is possible, and that it is therefore reasonable to suppose that the State must have been instituted for the good of the people, and not the people for the benefit of the State.

For Jones to think that Smith ought to pay taxes to educate his (Jones') children, and yet be indignant if someone suggests that on the same principle Brown ought to be made to pay for their shoes and hats.

For consistent Christians to uphold a system of education which takes no account of God and the spiritual part of the child's nature.

To ignore the fact that the great mass of the American people are Christians, and that Christian sentiments underlie their government, and keep in restraint the passions of the un-Christian mob.

To forget that the cause of this state of affairs is the Christian education which the founders of the country received.

The Correct Thing
In Reading

It is the Correct Thing

To remember that there are books and books and books.

Good books, bad books, instructive books, false books, frivolous books, corrupting books, senseless books, amusing books, edifying books, learned books, shallow books, coarse books, insidious books, sensational books, prosaic books, immoral books, spiritual books; books devoted to every "ology", science, art, fad, or foible under the sun.

That people read for pleasure, profit, or relaxation.

That as no one can read all the good books, even if life were a dozen times longer than it usually is, it would seem that sensible people would never be found not "passing the time", but wasting the time over books that are worthless or distinctly bad.

To have some system about one's reading if one would derive lasting profit from the books read.

To consider money spent for good books as money well invested.

For the average woman to examine her conscience well in regard to what she has read during her past life and to make a firm purpose of amendment.

To remember that a mind which is fed on newspapers, fashion magazines, sensational and trashy novels, to the exclusion of everything else, soon gets incapacitated for heavier and more wholesome food.

For a woman to make an inviolable rule never to read anything which she would be ashamed to acknowledge having read to the man whose good opinion she values most highly.

To lend a bad book, no matter how corrupted already the taste of the person soliciting it.

To burn any corrupting book which may happen to come into one's possession, either through ignorance of its nature when purchasing it, or in any other way.

To remember that one's library is an index to one's character.

To know that a taste for good reading can be cultivated.

To know that good novels may be both interesting and instructive.

That the great Cardinal Newman himself did not disdain a good novel.

To remember that novels are like mushrooms: they should be partaken of sparingly and great care used in their selection.

For each mind to select the food best suited to it, provided always that it is the best of its kind.

To remember that a few books well studied are more beneficial than a great many cursorily read.

To keep a note-book in which is entered every book and important article read during the year, with a short summary of their contents.

To know that Cardinal Newman, Gladstone, and many other great scholars practice this rule.

For cultivated Catholics to know the Catholic position in all the agitating questions of the day.

For parents to permit no books in their house which might have a demoralizing effect on their children.

To be as incensed at a person who recommends a bad book as at one who would mislead you into a mud hole.

To remember that as mud cannot fall on a white gown without leaving a stain, so neither can the mud of bad books fall on the soul without leaving a mark.

For American girls of a certain kind to remember that some of the noted French novelists whose works they so eagerly devour would no more permit their own daughters to read one of their books than they would allow them to enter a plague-stricken hospital.

To remember that there is a good deal of a fallacy in the much-quoted saying that "To the pure all things are pure," for practical demonstration has proven that mud is mud, disease is disease, no matter what angelic purity may characterize their victims. Of course some natures have an abnormal capacity for "getting soiled", just as some have constitutions for getting ill; but that fact does not lessen the muddiness of the mud, nor its tendency to leave a spot on whatever it touches.

It is Not the Correct Thing

To read any and every thing that may happen to fall in one's way.

To forget that to people of sense and intellectual resources the time generally passes all too quickly without any assistance in its flight from lurid or trashy books.

For girls to spend money for candy and toilet accessories and nothing for entertaining and instructive reading-matter.

For young men to indulge in every luxury excepting a library.

To forget that the frivolous girl passé now and that the cultivated one is to the front.

To imagine that age and ugliness are necessary adjuncts to learning.

To read anything which one would blush to be discovered in the act of reading.

To forget that those who lend or recommend bad books are accessory to another person's sin.

To believe that a body fed on adulterated food will become ill, but that a mind can be gorged on all sorts of trash and yet escape intellectual dyspepsia.

To forget that one is judged by the company one keeps, and that books are one's most constant companions.

To forget that the poison in some books is insidious and not easily discoverable to the novice.

To consult milliners and modistes about one's attire, and yet consider it not worth one's while to consult anybody about the books to read — the attire furnished for the mind.

For Catholics to be ignorant of the great books written by representative Catholics.

To imagine that Catholic periodicals can take a high rank without support.

To consider it no lack of cultivation to be ignorant of what Catholics have written and said about the great questions which agitate the intellectual world.

To expect the savant and the sage, the scientist and the writer, the tired matron and the frivolous girl, the mechanic and the clerk — all to be interested in the same class of books.

To imagine that one who reads everything that comes out is very brilliant or deeply learned.

To read a book only because it happens to be the fashion to do so.

To read without any system.

To keep no account of the books read.

To imagine that a person who extends the circulation of a bad book is not to blame for the damage done.

To allow questionable books in one's home.

To flatter one's self that one can read with impunity all sorts of books without experiencing any evil effects from the indulgence.

To forget that a mind can be kept healthy easier than it can be restored to health after once diseased.

To forget that a mind not already inclined to evil would take no pleasure in suggestive books, but would, on the contrary, be disgusted.

To ignore the advice and guidance of older, wiser, and more experienced persons in the serious matter of choosing proper books.

To neglect to subscribe for a Catholic newspaper or magazine.

To neglect to pay the subscription when due.

In Associating with Non-Catholics

It is the Correct Thing

To be willing and ready at all times and under all circumstances to give the reason for one's religious beliefs when asked to do so by a sincere seeker after truth.

To avoid argument merely for the sake of argument.

To say nothing needlessly to wound the feelings and religious opinions of those out of the Church.

To refute calumnies against the Church when they come under one's notice.

To remember that all minds cannot see alike; that certain minds unillumined by the grace of God are utterly unable to grasp religious truths which are perfectly clear to even a little child who has studied its Catechism faithfully.

To be firm always in one's adherence to the teachings of the Church, even at the risk of giving offence to others outside her pale.

To remember that "a liberal Catholic," in the sense in which the term is usually understood, is often no Catholic at all.

To know that right and wrong is a matter of conscience, even where one has a false conscience.

To know that a Catholic has no excuse for having a false conscience.

To know that ignorance is hardly an excuse for a Catholic, for there is every chance afforded for knowing the truth.

To know that it is forbidden for a Catholic to take part in any Protestant service under any circumstance.

To know that it is forbidden, not because there is any fear on the part of the Church that a well-instructed Catholic would be lead away from her fold, but because it is offering a gratuitous insult to God for a consistent Catholic to take part in a form of worship believed to be heretical, and another insult to the religious feelings of sincere members of the Church in question by reducing a religious service, very dear and sacred to them, to the level of a mere spectacle.

To remember that curiosity is not the proper motive in seeking the house of God.

To understand that whilst it would be wrong for a Catholic to go to a Protestant church, it is not wrong for a Protestant to go to a Catholic church, simply because it is one of the fundamental doctrines of all Protestant denominations that religion and religious opinions are very much a matter of private interpretation of the Bible; that two persons may belong to one church and yet not both believe exactly the same thing, and that all churches are alike pleasing to God in proportion to the sincerity of their members.

In brief, that the Catholic Church forbids her children to participate in religious services outside of her pale, and the Protestant churches leave their members to do as they please in the matter.

To know that Catholics visiting in non-Catholic families should be excused from taking part in the family prayers.

To participate in the grace said at table, if nothing is said contrary to the teaching of the Church in the form used.

To know that Catholics are excommunicated who marry before a Protestant minister.

To know that Catholics cannot officiate as bridesmaids or groomsmen at weddings solemnized in Protestant churches.

To know that it is not forbidden for Catholics to be present as spectators, merely, and as invited guests.

To know that Catholics cannot act as pallbearers at a funeral conducted by masonic lodges.

To remember that example is more powerful than precept.

It is Not the Correct Thing

To be unable to give a lucid explanation of one's belief.

To be fond of arguments and religious discussions.

To be careless about what one says, and the use of expressions calculated to give offence.

To weakly agree to slanders on the reputation and integrity of the Church or her ministers.

To manifest surprise and impatience at the failure of any one to grasp a truth that seems so plain to one's self.

To forget that whilst truth remains ever the same, the lamp of Faith, which is God's grace in the soul, may burn differently at different times and may even for some reason be withdrawn altogether; and that as a blind person cannot perceive the objects in the room, although the objects be there, so a soul left in darkness cannot perceive truth, although truth exists as plain as ever.

To imagine that because one cannot see a truth it is therefore not so.

For a Catholic to say that one Church is as good as another; for every intelligent Protestant knows that a consistent Catholic cannot think so, and that a Catholic who says he does is telling a deliberate falsehood.

To try to find excuses for doctrines which the Church never taught.

To go to a Protestant church and then neglect to mention the fact in confession, on the plea that one only went "to look on," "to pass away the time," to " listen to the music," "to see what it was all like," "because a friend desired it," etc., and not to take part in the service.

For Catholics to sing in Protestant churches.

To act in any way that would bring reproach on the Church or give scandal to those either in or out of the fold.

36

The Correct Thing
When Traveling in Foreign Countries

It is the Correct Thing

To remember that no duty and no passports are required for good manners, and that it would therefore be advisable to take them along with one.

To put one's conscience and one's worldly affairs in perfect order before sailing for foreign shores; for whilst travel has been rendered comparatively safe, accidents will happen on the best of regulated lines.

To remember that a severe case of seasickness brings out the ugly traits in one's character as effectively as hot tea brings out the measles.

To take for granted that the captain and officers of the ship know their duty, and that unsolicited advice will not be appreciated.

To remember that the caprices of the ocean and other causes give ample scope for the practice of resignation, patience, self-sacrifice, and other heroic virtues.

To be pleasant and genial with those one meets on shipboard, unless some notorious or particularly offensive person deserves to be considered the exception to the rule.

To be chary of forming friendships with chance traveling companions.

To remember that monopolists have no place on board a ship, and that the most comfortable places cannot be held exclusively by any one person.

To remember that Catholics have no more privilege to take part in Protestant worship on shipboard than they had on land!

To be willing and obliging in regard to taking part in theatricals and concerts gotten up on the ship for charity or merely for amusement.

To remember that even cultivated Americans can learn much by observation in Europe.

To be prepared to meet boors and miscellaneous cranks as well as agreeable and cultivated people.

To know all about the Inquisition, St. Bartholomew's day, Indulgences, and the other perennial springs of non-Catholic satisfaction, for the average tourist is required to take copious draughts at the *table d'hôte*, in the hotel drawing-rooms, and other places where travelers are thrown in contact with other travelers.

To understand that the deeds and misdeeds, the licentiousness and want of ability which characterized some of the Catholic kings were the results of human frailty and not of their religion.

To be able to explain intelligently that the Church does not claim either infallibility or impeccability for her children, and that she is not and should not in any justice be held responsible for the sins of individual members.

To understand that one can be patriotic and appreciative of one's own country without being offensive and abusive in regard to the countries of other people.

To remember that Europe and Europeans managed to exist fairly well for over a thousand years before America was even thought of.

To note the effects on the continent of the crusades of religious enlightenment which, according to Ruskin, every Briton who crosses the channel should help along.

To study the methods of the average Anglican crusader of a certain class, — the Briton who acts as an animated guide-book in matters of history to his chance traveling companions; who is fond of drawing parallels between England and other countries, always to the utter extinction of the other countries; who can demonstrate the problem to his own and the satisfaction of every true Briton, that Catholicity and crime are interchangeable terms, and that the "poverty and illiteracy" of continental countries are directly traceable to their religion, and that the natural resources of the country, the vast numbers of the inhabitants to be provided for, have nothing to do with the matter; the Briton who "pockets the candle because it was charged in the bill," appropriates the whole of a fowl in order to prevent the dulling of the cutlery in the act of carving it; who insists that the entire planetary system be stopped if the doing so would facilitate a journey for which he has paid; who calmly extinguishes the guide in his efforts to discharge his duties; discovers that the average Frenchman speaks barbarous French and not at all in accordance to rule; finds Vesuvius a rascally swindle, the Geneva Lakes a much vaunted humbug for the gratification of conscienceless hotel-keepers; gondolas in Venice beastly-uncomfortable; the Alps decidedly below par of what mountains should be that set themselves up as objects of interest; the wayside statues an insult to enlightened English Christianity; the contentment of the continental peasantry the most incontrovertible proof of their benighted condition; who rails at the want of liberty in Catholic countries, and nearly goes into apoplexy in places where Catholics are allowed the liberty to serve God according to their own ideas; who considers the fleas in Rome a providential visitation on the papal regime; the Briton who is so overcome with sympathy for the sufferings on the continent that he quite forgets all about the suffering right across St. George's Channel.

These and similar peculiarities the thoughtful tourist should note, not for imitation but for avoidance.

Since it is "meet and proper," and "quite the correct thing" to seek information when abroad, to find out from the Briton, who knows everything, why the notorious crimes and debaucheries of Henry VIII and his bar-sinister daughter Elizabeth, who were the recognized and legal heads and founders of the English Church, did not affect the purity and integrity of the doctrines of the Church — and why, on the other hand, the crimes real and alleged of some of the popes are proof positive of the corruption of the doctrines of the Catholic Church?

Why were the grand old churches in England, built by Catholics and owned by Catholics, seized and appropriated for use by the representatives of the English Church ?

Why is it right to steal a church and not right to steal anything else?

Why do English historians have so much to say about the persecutions of "Bloody Mary" and so little about the massacres of "Virgin Elizabeth," who calmly appropriated another woman's husband?

What was the exact number of the priests who were hanged,

drawn, and quartered at Tyburn, and the Catholic lay people who were treated in the same way ?

Why is it "meet, right, and most commendable" in England for the younger sons of "gentlemen" to enter orders and be presented in due time with the family living, regardless as to whether there is any aptitude or not for the ecclesiastical lot, and yet it be so dreadful a crime for parents on the continent to urge the ecclesiastical state on their children ?

Why is the Catholic Church held to teach that licentiousness, theft, and oppression are right because Catholic kings sometimes practiced those vices, and the English Church not held as teaching the same thing, when not only Protestant kings, but English kings, the very heads of the Church itself, were guilty of the same crimes and worse?

Does crossing the Channel make fish for Protestants become fowl for Catholics?

Why is the code of morality so much lower in Protestant Scotland than it is in Catholic Spain?

Why is poverty in Italy considered the direct results of the papal government having been so long in power, and the poverty and almost indescribable suffering in Ireland considered as a thing quite apart from the Hanoverian dynasty?

Why are Protestants so anxious to force their religion upon people who do not want it, and so indifferent to the wants of the thousands of people right in London, the "center of the civilized world," who have no religion at all?

Why has London, in proportion to size, more crime than any other city in Europe?

Why is the brutal degradation which statisticians have found in some of the mining districts of England viewed as among the unavoidable things, and yet the mere lack of the ability to read and write considered as the direct result of bad Catholic governments on the continent ?

To find out for the benefit of future historians where the documents can be obtained which prove that the popes made a traffic of indulgences, used the papal power to oppress the weak, and authorized the dark crimes which are imputed to them.

To find out why the Church preserved the Sacred Scriptures for nearly two thousand years, if she is afraid of their influence on her children.

Why Catholics founded the Universities of Oxford, Heidelberg, Padua, Douai, Salamanca, and scores of others, if the Church be the foe to education?

In return for so much information, to be willing to give one's informant any little knowledge which may happen to lie in one's power.

To be well versed in history, both sacred and profane, before going abroad.

To remember that guide-books often err.

To remember that the churches and galleries and palaces of Europe were not built exactly and solely for the pleasure and benefit of tourists.

To be reasonable, if one can afford it, in the matter of fees.

To remember that pious legends are not matters of faith, although a great many of them are authenticated and worthy of belief.

To remember that it is only the courteous thing to leave pecuniary mementos in the churches and convents, the visiting of which afforded one pleasure and profit.

To remember that thanks and apologies cost nothing, and are among the outward signs which indicate good breeding.

To remember that it is not always necessary to express one's opinion about a thing which is not altogether pleasing to one's fancy.

To remember that tourists are not sent abroad to instruct foreigners as to their own ignorance or the shortcomings of their country.

To insist that those in one's party show proper reverence in the churches visited.

To remember that a falsehood elsewhere does not become mere prevarication in the custom-house.

To remember when with supercilious foreigners that if America has no great pictures, she at least holds the patent on the most perfect plough in the world.

To desist, for the sake of a long-suffering public, from writing a book of "European Impressions" on one's return.

It is Not the Correct Thing

To imagine that a woman will be mistaken for a lady if she does not act as one.

To think that the practice of the Christian virtues should be suspended on sea.

To forget that patient endurance and a lemon are the best antidotes for seasickness.

To imagine that chance auditors are vitally interested in one's physical condition, and to therefore inflict a minute account of all the stages of *mal de mer* on them.

To forget to say one's night and morning prayers.

For a gentleman (?) to imagine that profanity on shipboard is a gentlemanly accomplishment.

To join in any religious services held by a Protestant minister on shipboard.

To be ignorant as to whether the charges made against the Church are true or false.

To try to explain to tourists what one does not understand one's self.

To eat meat on Friday when traveling, if one is not ill and there is no necessity for so doing.

To judge cultivated and enlightened Protestants by the blustering Briton one meets everywhere on the continent of Europe.

To seek religious discussions when traveling.

To inflict one's society on those who evidently do not appreciate it.

To imagine that there is nothing ill-bred in visiting foreign convents and then ridiculing their inmates.

To compare the monk who kindly acts as one's guide to a cow, as did a certain strong-minded and distinguished lady from Massachusetts.

To forget the customary fees to guides, vergers, etc.

For Catholic girls to imitate *Miss Daisy Miller.*[13]

After one's return to make use of the phrase "when I was in Europe" more than ten times a day.

To ape foreign manners and thus become ridiculous.

To imagine that one is to be pitied who has not been "abroad."

To forget that, after all, "there is no place like home."

---

13 *Miss Daisy Miller* was a novella by Henry James (1878). Part romantic comedy, part social commentary, and a mockery of rich, snobby Americans who tried to imitate rich, snobby Europeans.

37

The Correct Thing
For Special Devotions

It is the Correct Thing

To remember that for each day of the week there is a special devotion.

Sunday, the Holy Trinity.

Monday, the Souls in Purgatory.

Tuesday, the Guardian Angels.

Wednesday, St. Joseph.

Thursday, the Blessed Sacrament.

Friday, the Sacred Heart and the Passion.

Saturday, the Blessed Virgin.

That the months are also consecrated to particular devotions, the most generally observed being:

March, St. Joseph.

May, the Blessed Virgin.

June, the Sacred Heart.

July, the Precious Blood.

October, the Guardian Angels and the Rosary.

November, the Souls in Purgatory.

To hear Mass, or perform some work of devotion, on the feastday of one's patron saint.

To congratulate clergymen and members of religious communities on their names-days; that is, the feast days of their patron saints.

To know that in Catholic countries the names-days are celebrated as well as the birthdays.

To know that the patronal feast of a country is always a day of obligation: as the feast of the Immaculate Conception" in the United States, St. Patrick in Ireland, St. Boniface in Germany, St. James in Spain, St. George in England, etc.

To pray to St. Joseph for money.

To St. Anthony for things that are lost or misplaced.

To St. Aloysius, the patron of youth, for assistance in studies and the virtue of purity.

To St. Cecilia, the patroness of musicians, for success in musical studies.

To St. Thomas Aquinas, patron of philosophers, for a clear understanding of philosophical and theological questions.

To St. Roche for the restoration of health, and when a plague is threatened.

To St. Blase for a cure of all diseases of the throat.

To St. Anne, mother of the Blessed Virgin and patroness of married women, for all the graces and assistance necessary in the matrimonial state.

To St. Catherine for a husband.

To St. Patrick, the great apostle of Ireland, for conversions.

For those who desire the protection and assistance of St. Aloysius, to "make the Aloysius Sundays"; that is, to approach Holy Communion on the six Sundays preceding his Feast — the 21st of June.

To know that by approaching Holy Communion on the five Sundays preceding the feast of St. Francis of Assisi, — October 4th, — a plenary indulgence may be gained on each Sunday.

To know that in all churches belonging to the Franciscans, as well as in all churches and chapels in which the Third Order of St. Francis is canonically established, the same indulgences can be gained as are attached to the Church of the Portiuncula in Rome, by following the same conditions: namely, confession and Holy Communion and six visits to the Church, praying for the intention of the Holy Father and the welfare of the Church, on the Feast of the Portiuncula, the 2nvd of August, between the hours of sunrise and sunset. (Plenary indulgence applicable to the souls in Purgatory.)

To make a novena, that is, the nine days' prayer, by way of preparation for the great feastdays in the year.

If this novena is public in the church, to be punctual in attendance, and to arrive in time.

If absolutely impossible to make the novena in the church, to do so at home, having a stated hour each day for saying the prayers.

For persons in the world who desire to lead a more perfect life than they have hitherto done to join the Third Order of St. Francis. [This order was founded by St. Francis at the earnest solicitation of some pious people who wished to lead a more perfect Christian life without abandoning any of their ordinary avocations in the world. Application for membership may be made to any Franciscan priest, or to others to whom they have delegated authority. The habit consists only of the scapular and cord worn under the ordinary apparel; the obligations are to perform certain works of devotion, none of them incompatible with worldly duties; the rewards are a great many indulgences and spiritual favors.]

For all Catholics worthy of the name to join the League of the Sacred Heart.

To know that this is a society which owes its origin to the Blessed Margaret Mary, a Visitation nun in France. That it is divided into three degrees: The first degree comprises all the associates who pledge themselves simply to make an offering at their morning prayers of all their works, prayers, and sufferings of the day, for the honor of the Sacred Heart. The second degree is composed of those who unite to say one decade of the Rosary daily for the intentions of the League. The third degree comprises those who undertake to make a monthly or weekly reparation to the Sacred Heart.

To know that the first Friday of the month is consecrated especially to the Sacred Heart, and that all members of the League should make their Communion of Reparation on that day.

To know that a plenary indulgence may be gained on that day on the usual conditions.

To wear a scapular of the Sacred Heart and also to have a picture of the Sacred Heart in one's room.

To subscribe for the "Messenger of the Sacred Heart," if one desires to be informed of the work the League is doing, and to keep alive the spirit of piety.

To know that in nearly all parishes a League or Confraternity of the Sacred Heart exists, and that there is no expense and no ceremony required for admission.

For those piously inclined to act as promoters.

For those who can possibly do so, to "make the nine Fridays;" that is, approach Holy Communion on the first Friday of every month for nine consecutive months.

To know that if one misses a Friday, no matter for what reason, the nine must be begun again.

To join the Guard of Honor. [That is, a band who pledge themselves to spend one hour each day in spiritual union with the Sacred Heart. It includes no duty excepting to make the intention at the beginning of the hour to honor the Sacred Heart in whatever one may be doing at the time, whether studying, working, or even walking. In convents, and by some pious people in the world, the Hour of Guard is passed before the Blessed Sacrament. Even people who are not very pious manage sometimes to spend a part of their hour in the church.]

For all men who feel any compassion for the poor to join the St. Vincent de Paul Society.

For young ladies to become "Daughters of the Queen."

For young ladies to belong to a Sodality of the Blessed Virgin, either at their parish church or in connection with one of the convents, many of which have sodalities for the benefit of their old pupils and others.

For young men to remember that sodalities exist for them quite as well as for their sisters.

For married ladies to belong to the Sodality of St. Anne.

For all those who honor the name of Our Lord to join the Holy Name Society.

For men and boys addicted to the horrible vice of swearing to be punctilious in their attendance at the meetings of this society.

For all persons, whether members of the society or not, to make an act of reparation in their hearts when they hear the Sacred Name taken in vain.

For pious Catholics of both sexes, and all ages and conditions, to join the Confraternity of the Holy Face.

To know that the object of this society is to honor the suffering Face of Our Redeemer, imprinted on the veil of Veronica, and to repair by acts of devotion and penance the outrages offered in these days of impiety to the majesty of God.

For the members to recite daily one *Pater, Ave,* and *Gloria,* and the invocation, "Lord, show us Thy Face and we shall be saved."

To wear an image of the Holy Face either on a medal, cross, or scapular.

If convenient, to attend the monthly meetings.

To extend the devotion as far as lies in one's power.

To have one's name inscribed on the register of the association.

For Catholics who ever expect to go to Purgatory, or who have any relatives and friends there, or who feel any compassion for the sufferings of others, to join the Purgatorian Society.

For Catholics who desire to see the altar of God adorned and taken care of, to join the Altar Society.

To pay one's dues after joining.

To remember that the greatest women, royalty itself, have always been proud to work for the altar. The daughter of an emperor, Isabella of Brazil, scrubbed the church more than once and was always an active member of the Altar Society.

For every Catholic, from the time he reaches the age of reason — usually at seven years — until the hour of his death, to wear the Brown Scapular.

To know that the Brown Scapular, or little habit of the Blessed Virgin, is composed of two square pieces of brown woolen cloth, connected by two cords and designed to be worn over the shoulders, hence the name scapular, from *scapulae*, shoulders. According to tradition, it was given to St. Simon Stock, General of the Carmelite Order, on the 16th of July, 1251, by the Blessed Virgin herself.

To know that one must be invested in the scapular by a priest having the authority to do so.

To know that when one's scapulars wear out one need not be enrolled again: simply procure a pair of new ones and put them on, and then burn the old ones. (Anything that has been blessed should always be burned, never thrown away.)

To know that a person may be enrolled with the scapulars of another person.

To know that the picture or embroidery, whilst conducting to devotion, is not necessary to the integrity of the scapulars.

If one desires to do so, to cover scapulars with linen cases, in which may also be worn medals, an *Agnus Dei*, and other pious objects.

To know that one who wears the Brown Scapular becomes a sharer in the prayers and good works of the Carmelite Order, but that if it is desired to gain all the numerous indulgences seven Our Fathers and seven Hail Marys must be recited daily, and, some writers say, abstain from meat on Wednesdays and Saturdays.

For those who wear the scapular to approach Holy Communion on the Feast of Mount Carmel — July 16th.

To be enrolled in the Five Scapulars if the opportunity offers.

The four others, beside the Scapular of Mount Carmel, are the Scapular of the Holy Trinity, white linen with a red cross; seven dolors, black woolen stuff; Immaculate Conception, light blue woolen; scapular of the Passion, red woolen. Only priests having special faculties can enroll in the Five Scapulars, generally given to the Regular Clergy.

To know that there are many indulgences attached to the wearing of the Five Scapulars

To recite the *Angelus* morning, noon, and night.

> The angel of the Lord declared unto Mary;
> R. And she conceived by the Holy Ghost. Hail Mary, etc.
> Behold the handmaid of the Lord;
> R. Be it done unto me according to thy word. Hail Mary, etc.
> The Word was made Flesh,
> R. And dwelt amongst us. Hail Mary, etc.
> Prayer. — Pour forth, we beseech Thee, O Lord, Thy grace into our hearts, that we to whom the Incarnation of Christ Thy Son was made known by the message of an angel may, by His passion and cross, be brought to the glory of His Resurrection; through the same Christ Our Lord. Amen.

To kneel at the *Angelus* excepting on Sunday.

On Sunday to stand, bending the knee only at the last part to adore the Incarnation.

To recite the *Regina Coeli* instead of the *Angelus* during Eastertide; that is, from Holy Saturday until Trinity Sunday.

For those who wish to do so to use the rhythmical form of the *Regina Coeli*.

> Rejoice, O Queen of Heaven, to see. Alleluia!
> The sacred Infant born of thee. Alleluia!
> Spring up in glory from the tomb. Alleluia!
> Oh, by thy prayers prevent our doom. Alleluia!
> Rejoice and be glad, O Virgin Mary. Alleluia!
> Because Our Lord is truly risen. Alleluia!
> Prayer. — O God, Who through the resurrection of Thy Son Our Lord Jesus Christ hast vouchsafed to fill the world with joy, grant, we beseech Thee, that by the intercession of the Virgin Mary, His Mother, we may receive the joys of eternal life. Through the same Christ Our Lord. Amen.

In passing a church, for men to lift their hats and for women to make the sign of the cross.

To make a practice of reading some religious book every day for a few minutes at least. There are a number of excellent little books for the beginners in spiritual perfection, divided into short paragraphs containing counsels, exhortations, or lives of the saints.

To subscribe for a good Catholic paper, and to read it when it comes every week. Religious reading is homeopathic in its effects— a little constantly repeated will make an impression after a time on the most careless of hearts.

To remember that one may belong to a great many societies and fulfill all the requirements laid down for ordinary Christians in a very small portion of time — scarcely as much as is devoted to the morning paper. To make a cursory estimate: Sodality, half an hour twice a month; decade of the Rosary, five minutes; morning offering to the Sacred Heart, one minute; spiritual reading, five minutes; ejaculations, about thirty seconds each; Communion on the first Friday, one hour a month; confession and preparation for Communion, one hour per month; *Angelus*, two minutes each time — six minutes per day; morning and evening prayers, more or less lengthy (more or less brief might be more correct), according to one's piety; an occasional visit to the Blessed Sacrament; and adding all the time spent in acts of devotion, the amount remains surprisingly small, especially when compared with the amount wasted in gossip or ways that are worse.

To know that this estimate is intended for the primary grades in Christian perfection.

To remember that one of the most meritorious acts a person can perform, an act in the power of everybody or nearly everybody, is to daily assist at the Holy Sacrifice of Mass. People who have any claims to piety hear Mass as often as they possibly can.

To remember that it is better to say a few prayers well than a great many carelessly.

To know that the priests of a parish are always willing to give all necessary information about the devotional societies which one may wish to join.

38

The Correct Thing
In Regard to the Rosary

It is the Correct Thing

To have a Rosary blessed before using.

To have the intention when saying it to gain the indulgences applied to the blessed Rosary.

To decide on an object for which to pray before beginning.

To offer the Rosary for our Holy Father, our bishop, our rector, our confessor, our relatives and friends, for the conversion of sinners, the welfare of the Catholic Church, and for the souls in Purgatory.

To become a member of the society of the Holy Rosary, if established in one's parish.

To always carry a Rosary in one's pocket, and to say it when traveling, and when not engaged otherwise away from home.

To remember that a muff in winter enables a lady to say her Rosary without observation.

To remember that beads made of glass or other brittle material cannot be indulgenced.[14]

To know that the indulgences attached to a Rosary are gained by the first person receiving it for use.

To know that an owner of an indulgenced Rosary in use cannot transfer Rosary with indulgence to another person.

To know that one may lend a Rosary to another, but cannot lend the indulgence.

To know that if one lends a Rosary that another may gain the indulgence, the Rosary loses all indulgence and must be blessed again.

To know that one may oblige another by lending a Rosary, provided there is no intention to transfer the indulgence.

Or if one's Rosary is used without the owner's knowledge, the indulgence is not lost.

To know that the indulgence is attached to the Rosary and not to the owner; hence if the indulgenced Rosary is lost, one cannot supply its place by another not blessed.

To know that a blessed Rosary cannot be sold without losing its blessing.

To know that if one is commissioned to procure a Rosary and have it blessed for another, he can demand the amount expended in the purchase without prejudice to the indulgenced Rosary.

---

14   Because if it breaks, small shards of blessed Rosary may be lost.

To know that a broken bead here and there may be renewed without losing the indulgence.

To know that the cross and five beads usually attached to a Rosary do not form an essential part; hence if they are lost or broken, the indulgence remains.

To know that several kinds of indulgences may be attached to the same Rosary. It is probable that each kind should have its special intention, as all the kinds of indulgences are not gained by one act.

To know that by custom the recipient of a blessed Rosary says the first for the wants of the Church, second for the pope, and the third for the one who blessed it.

It is Not the Correct Thing

To buy a Rosary and neglect to have it blessed at once.

To neglect to obtain certain indulgences when the opportunity offers.

To neglect or refuse to become a member of the parish Rosary society.

To omit the daily recitation of one decade if a member of the Rosary society.

To neglect to repair one's Rosary, or to get a new one when broken.

To omit to carry a blessed Rosary on one's person.

To barter one's indulgenced Rosary for money or valuables.

To say the Rosary without devotion or in a hurry.

To omit reflection upon the mysteries while saying the Rosary.

To be ashamed to carry a Rosary or to recite it with others in common.

To imagine that the Rosary is a form of prayer for the use of old people or those not able to read.

To be satisfied on occasion to say the Rosary on one's fingers: this, however, is better than nothing.

To borrow the Rosary of another when one can easily get his own.

To ask the use of a Rosary which is known to have special indulgences attached to it.

To buy from peddlers what they falsely assert are indulgenced rosaries from the Holy Land or elsewhere.

To have one's Rosary blessed by every strange priest one meets.

To think that there is any special merit for a lazy Christian to hang a Rosary upon his bedpost when he might keep it in a more accessible place, such as his pocket.

To exchange rosaries in order to exchange the indulgences attached to each. (Both rosaries lose any indulgence they may have when this is done.)

39

The Correct Thing
In Saying the Rosary

It is the Correct Thing

To recite the Apostles' Creed on the crucifix attached to the Rosary.

On the large bead the *Gloria* and Our Father.

On the three small beads three Hail Marys. On the first with the invocation "Increase my faith"; on the second, "Strengthen my hope"; on the third, "Inflame my heart with the fire of Divine love".

To know that the fifteen decades which constitute the whole Rosary are divided into three parts, to be recited on different days.

The five Joyful Mysteries

For Mondays and Thursdays, the Sundays of Advent, and from the Epiphany until Lent.

> 1st. The Annunciation. [The Angel Gabriel announced to the Blessed Virgin that she would be the Mother of God.]
> 2dn. The Visitation. [The Blessed Virgin pays a visit to her cousin, St. Elizabeth, before the birth of St. John.]
> 3rd. The Nativity. [The birth of Our Saviour in a stable at Bethlehem.]
> 4th. The Presentation. [The Blessed Virgin on the day of her purification presented the Child Jesus in the Temple, where holy Simeon gave thanks and received Him in his arms.]
> 5th. The finding of Jesus in the Temple. [The Blessed Virgin lost her Beloved Son in Jerusalem, and having searched for Him three days, found Him in the Temple in the midst of the Doctors, hearing them and asking them questions.]

The Sorrowful Mysteries

For Tuesdays and Fridays and Sundays in Lent.

> 1st. The Agony in the Garden. [Our Lord praying in the Garden of Olives was so overcome with anguish that He sweat blood.
> 2nd. The Scourging. [Our Lord was bound to a pillar and scourged in the house of Pilate.]
> 3rd. The Crowning with Thorns. [The Jews placed a crown of thorns on the Sacred Brow, pressing it into the flesh, and mocked Him, crying, " Hail, King of the Jews !"]
> 4th. The Carrying of the Cross. [Jesus, being condemned to death, was forced to carry His cross to Calvary.]
> 5th. The Crucifixion. [Our Lord was nailed to the cross and crucified between two thieves, suffering His agony for three hours.]

The Glorious Mysteries

For Wednesdays and Saturdays, and the Sundays from Easter until Advent

> 1st. The Resurrection. [Our Lord arose the third day from the tomb, the first Easter.]
>
> 2nd. The Ascension. [Forty days after the Resurrection Our Lord ascended into heaven in the presence of the Blessed Virgin and His Apostles.]
>
> 3rd. The Descent of the Holy Ghost [Ten days after His ascension Our Lord sent the Holy Ghost on His Apostles in the form of fiery tongues, after which they separated to fulfill their missions in the different parts of the world.]
>
> 4th. The Assumption. [Our Lady died twelve years after the resurrection of her Divine Son, and her body was assumed into heaven by angels.]
>
> 5th. The Coronation. [The Blessed Virgin was crowned the Queen of heaven by her Son.]

A pious and laudable custom prevails in many families to add to the ordinary Rosary one decade for the suffering souls in Purgatory.

There's nothing in the world like etiquette,
In kingly chambers or imperial halls,
As also at the race and county balls.

Lord Byron

Etiquette. The dictionary tells us that this stuffy-sounding French word is the one we now use to mean a code of ethical behavior, decorum, or good manners. In other words, morally good inner character traits that are exhibited in an outward manner.

But today, the idea of etiquette has taken on the form of weakness. If a man acts chivalrous, he may be seen as effeminate. Would it be better for society— or for a man's soul — if he acted selfish, arrogant, and boorish?

So when did the idea of etiquette, decorum, or having an internal code of manners garner such a bad reputation? Why do people resist 'good manners' so much? Is it because we have seen a shift to a self-centered individualistic society? Many people seem to have a contempt for authority and want to do their own thing. "Who is to say what is good manners?" they claim. Is it that they are insecure and want to be unique by coming up with their own inner code of what is good, proper, and polite? Or a loss of respect for others?

Encouraging good character is timeless and a matter of Natural Law. All cultures, races, and sophists have taught that there is a set, internal character that is lived out in an external manner — a way for a group of people living together to maintain social order.

In society, good manners are founded on reason and common sense — for the individual good, and for the greater common good. It's the 'code' that binds society together for the betterment of all so that people with various backgrounds, motives, and goals can live in harmony. "A man's manners are his fortune," as the old saying goes.

About 5,000 years ago, an Egyptian official wrote *The Maxims of Ptahhotep*, which encouraged appropriate interpersonal behaviors such as truthfulness, self-control, and kindness towards others. Scholars think that, historically, it was the first book in print -- and your can still find it on bookshelves. Think about that: The first book in print was about good manners.

Plato taught the virtues of temperance, prudence, courage and justice. And in the Nicomachean Ethics, Aristotle says that virtues are morally good inner character traits that are exhibited in an outward manner. The golden mean of a virtuous act is, "at the right times, about the right things, towards the right people, for the right end, and in the right way".

In eighteenth century France, Louis XVI entertained at The Palace of Versailles and codified a system of etiquette that became a sign of being a genteel member of society. In England, the eloquent Edmund Burke wrote that, "Manners are of more importance than laws. Upon them, in a great measure, the laws depend." The influential philosopher Lord Shaftesbury wrote a series of articles on politeness and argued that virtue leads to happiness. His writings exerted an enormous influence throughout the eighteenth and nineteenth centuries as more articles, books, and clubs established rules and procedures meant to reform manners and morals for the betterment of self and society.

By the Victorian era, good manners and etiquette developed into almost an obsession of rules. The intent for many faded away from morality and virtue, and 'good manners and breeding' became a means for social advancement and class division. Could this be where "etiquette" started to get a bad name? Lost was the understanding that manners, courtesy, and decorum helps reduce the friction that dealing with others in this vale of tears brings on a daily basis. Lost was acknowledging that a 'set code' of decorum allows us to move throughout society, with all the conflicting motives. Lost was the idea of manners being a virtue.

Fundamentally, charity and good manners are Natural Law — the Truth that ignites the inner life of man.

The Old Testament provides us with the Ten Commandments. Our Catechism teaches the four Cardinal Virtues (prudence, justice, fortitude, and temperance) and the three Theological Virtues (faith, hope and charity). What does the Bible say is the greatest of these? Charity, which is patient and kind. Charity is content (not envious), humble (not boastful), unpretentious (not ambitious), unselfish (not seeketh their own), cheerful (not provoked to anger), and is positive (thinketh no evil). (See 1 Corinthians 13.)

Doesn't the Biblical definition of charity sound like 'morally good inner character traits that are exhibited in an outward manner'?

Manners are the virtue of charity. Jesus himself said that we should treat others the way we want to be treated (St. Matthew 7:12), and the entire Epistle of St. James is a primer in manners.

Good manners, decorum, charity, and etiquette benefits not only us personally, but the entire society. Good manners show an inner character that the ancients called "virtues" — those morally good inner character traits that are exhibited in an outward manner. That's why there really is no such thing as "company manners". Our everyday manners at home, at work, in school, and at Mass reflect our inner character. And sadly, character is in short supply these days. It is my hope that this little handbook with help replenish that supply.

Colleen M. Hammond
Easter Monday, April 21, 2014

Made in the USA
Charleston, SC
26 March 2014